mindful vegan meals

mindful vegan meals

food is
YOUR FRIEND

Maria Koutsogiannis

FOUNDER OF FOODBYMARIA

PAGE STREET
PUBLISHING CO.

PAGE STREET
PUBLISHING CO.

First published in 2018 by
Page Street Publishing Co.
27 Congress Street, Suite 105
Salem, MA 01970
www.pagestreetpublishing.com

Distributed by Macmillan, sales in Canada by The Canadian Manda Group.

22 21 20 19 18   1 2 3 4 5

ISBN-13: 978-1-62414-575-9

ISBN-10: 1-62414-575-2

Library of Congress Control Number: 2017962444

Cover and book design by Page Street Publishing Co.

Photography by Maria Koutsogiannis and on pages 2, 5, 6, 10, 15, 16, 76, 100, 108, 149, 150, 154, 175, 176, 194, 198, 200, 202 and 204 by Chris Amat

Printed and bound in the United States

Dedication

To my teenage self, your confusion and hardships led to me being the strongest, most confident version of myself.

To women and men who still suffer with self-confidence issues, body dysmorphia or eating disorders. Your struggles mean something, keep listening and you will find your answer. Never give up. You deserve the world because you are enough.

To Andrew, for helping me fight that bitch of a disease and for helping me see what I couldn't for years.

To my mom and dad for raising an outspoken woman, the war against myself would have been lost without the strength and strong will you bestowed to me.

To my friends and extended family, thank you for following my journey and joining me on this ever-changing road.

Contents

My Story

I still can't believe that people all over the world are reading my first published book—*Mindful Vegan Meals*. I can't believe it. Even as I write the opening paragraph for this book, I still cannot come to terms with the fact that I have achieved one of my biggest dreams. And I did it with the help of my followers, family and friends. You might not be familiar with me or my blog, FoodByMaria, but don't worry, I am going to introduce myself. If you're a friend, follower or fan then you know this is a very emotional and important time in my life. I wrote my first book and am able to share my story with the world, through recipes and experiences. Thank you.

Let's backtrack. Back to the days of thirteen-year-old Maria. The figure skater and track athlete, the overtalker, the "lesser than" popular girl at school—in my eyes, anyway. I was so many things but I was one thing that has always stood out to myself: I was a dreamer. I was also very critical, a perfectionist (I have obsessive-compulsive disorder—OCD). I also went 100% if I decided I wanted something. All these characteristics, for me, were a recipe for potential and utter disaster, but I'll tell you more about that later.

There is one significant thing in my life that impacted a lot of other things. On Sept 19, 2004, my family and I were in a horrific car accident on the way home from a family wedding. I remember every distinct detail from the crash but what I remember most was the still silence before realizing exactly what had just happened. We had just rolled, four times, on the highway, going the slightest bit over the speed limit. My mind was in shambles as I desperately tried to put together the puzzle pieces.

As the emergency crew and bystanders flocked to our vehicle all I could hear was "How many survivors?" and "Are you okay?" To be honest, at that point I did not even notice them—I just wanted to find my sister, who had been thrown from the car. Once I saw she was OK I proceeded to yell for my brother. He was fine. I yelled for my mom, she was ok, then I yelled for my dad and he was OK, too. This day could have been much worse but for some reason no one was hurt and we were left on this earth to continue our lives.

For me, our survival meant so much more. I never talked about this with anyone when I was young because saying it to myself was weird enough. I believe I lived because I was put on this planet to do something beautiful. I knew that something big was meant for me but I didn't know what that was. I just knew that whatever it was, I would be able to help change the world.

After the accident, the world around me kept turning, I went on to graduate from high school and moved to Calgary to study business at Mount Royal University. Before I moved to Calgary, I went through a weird phase in the spring and around high school graduation. I had just had ACL surgery after an injury in track and field and had lost loads of weight. The weight loss slowly turned into an obsession and as the summer approached, I realized I had become fixated on my weight loss and desperately wanted to stay skinny forever.

At first, it was difficult adapting to university. I didn't have my family and my old routine and I really didn't know anyone but my good friend, Whit. Three months into university things started to blur, both mentally and physically. I was falling into a small depression; I was drinking far too often and I really missed my hometown, Swift Current. Because of all this I was also putting on a bit of weight—I didn't have my mom feeding me every day nor did I have someone telling me that I probably shouldn't be getting drunk four nights a week. My lifestyle changed quite a bit but it was about to change for the worse, really soon.

Sometime in November I was standing in the bathroom, looking at myself in the mirror. I was wearing a pair of jeans, a burgundy top and a little hoodie. I felt super bloated, I was so unhappy that I had put on the amount of weight that I had and genuinely began to hate myself and the life I was living. I looked into the toilet and got down on my knees. Somewhere between fucked up and very confused I managed to convince myself that it was a good idea to shove two fingers down my throat. I will never, ever forget the first time. My brain was screaming at me "MARIA DON'T!" but my heart knew; it knew that if I did this then maybe I would feel better and that I would be able to get on with my life knowing that I had an escape from the world.

In the beginning the addiction wasn't so bad, but as the days, months and years went on it continued to get worse. I would always sit down for a meal and think to myself "where is the nearest bathroom?" before I would even take a bite. I was going to vomit and no matter what happened I would make sure that I did. I didn't feel comfortable with food in my stomach because I didn't trust food, not to mention understand it. Let's not forget that at this point in my life I was unhappy with my weight so I truly thought vomiting would help me keep the pounds off.

I could not have been more wrong. Want to know why I know that? Well, because, at one point in my bulimic life I actually ended up getting caught by someone I used to call a friend. I got a text one Sunday night saying, "You forgot to flush." Before I could even explain myself, I was already getting text messages from my three best friends. I had never felt more betrayed, sad and embarrassed in my life. So, long story short, once I was outed to my friends that I was still sick after I'd told them I was doing better I was basically forced to try and *actually* get better.

Getting better. How do you do that? Before I move on with my rant and talk about how I started to get better I just want to say 1) I love my best friends and am so thankful they were there for me when I wasn't there for myself and 2) *Never ever* send text messages about people's vomit to their best friends if they actually have a disease/addiction. I realize now that that person was only trying to help me but in reality it made everything ten times worse, in my head anyway. When someone suffers from bulimia, anorexia or binge eating it's often because they have a hidden or obvious issue such as OCD or self-esteem issues, so trying to help them by text-shaming them isn't going to make things easier. I'm not even sure why I am telling you this story but part of me feels like I need to. Not for you. For me. I've been keeping these feelings swept away under my neck vertebrae for years, they're weighing me down and I think for the sanity of my own mind and healing it helps knowing that I acknowledge that this moment was the lowest point in my entire bulimic experience.

I admit I was wrong for lying to my friends and relapsing.

I admit I was trying to get better but everything I fucking tried didn't work.

I admit I should have gone to the doctor. Or even tried to get myself help.

I admit it.

I get it.

But throughout this whole 6-year hell storm, I promise you I tried my hardest to be a good member of society.

Where am I going with this? Be a good human. Be kind. I guarantee that there are people, every day, who are going through what I went through and all they need is your patience. I'm not saying not to help them or become angry when they lie, or continue to hurt themselves. I am saying that the disease has taken control over them and their actions often aren't theirs.

I'm sorry to those I hurt while sick, but I killed that bitch, just like all of you out there suffering will one day too.

Once I got better I started eating normal meals again and keeping them down. Problem was, the meals I was eating were way too big, way too often and way too carb-heavy. I packed on the pounds quickly, developed some pretty intense constipation and basically looked like the cutest Pillsbury Dough boy ever except I was super unhappy. Before I knew it, I fell back into the bad routine and continued being sick for a while longer.

It was never the case that I was afraid of food, that was obvious, but it was rather complicated at times because I would find myself eating just to be sick. I would sometimes eat, vomit, then eat again. I would dream about my next meal and the addiction just continued to get worse because I really, truly, loved food; I just had no clue what it was doing to my body and why it was changing so much. This was really conflicting. I have always been very passionate about food and it broke my heart when my sickness got so bad I couldn't even talk about it anymore. And there was the other problem . . . when I let it completely consume my thoughts I would begin counting calories. Was I nuts? Maria, you are bulimic. Why are you counting when you know very damn well that it is going to end up in the bottom of a toilet?

Isn't it strange how the one thing I was afraid of most is now the driver to all my happiness and success? What changed? What did I do differently? I educated myself. I cut the crap, went back to basics and taught myself everything I needed to know from the ground up about food and how I would have a relationship with it for the rest of my life. A lot of people ask me, nearly every day, how did you change your relationship with food? Well I started in the most obvious but most unwanted and darkest part of the story. I started with the relationship I had with myself and that damn devil demon in the mirror—I am referring here to my subconscious. The less strong, easily manipulated and distorted human being who let me believe I wasn't enough.

It was all baby steps from the beginning. Things like going to the bathroom with the door open after eating to hold myself accountable. I would blow my nose or cough while I was on the toilet to signal to my boyfriend, Andrew, that I was indeed peeing. Doing so made me feel better because we were at the early stages of our relationship and I deeply wanted to strengthen the trust and bond Andrew and I had. Slowly, as the days and months went on I no longer thought about being sick.

Leaving my meals in the toilet was a thing of the past and I quickly started to focus on positive nutrition and getting my body and mind right. It all came down to those damn plants, I tell you. I was eating more vegetables than an herbivore and I felt really good. Like *really* good. I had fewer digestive issues, I felt light on my feet and started to get that thirteen-year-old's energy back!

This is where my plant-based lifestyle was born. I realized that without meat, dairy and processed foods I could finally get that body I always wanted but without the societal pressures. It was what *I* wanted and I was doing it for *me*.

Eating plant-based has been so fun and adventurous. I have found a way to utilize it so I have a better connection with food and am not worried about the dishes and meals I eat because eating plants is always good for you!

Did I mention I am not longer afraid of carbs? I do not even think twice about pizza, burgers, sandwiches or pasta. I simply eat them, appreciate their benefits and move the hell on. I eat meals that society shames and makes us feel bad for (even the plant-based versions) and yet I continue to be the strongest, smallest and most confident I have ever been! I know my food education and self-love is attributed to these changes but I would be lying if I didn't credit my diet—duh!

Eating plant-based is not easy at the beginning but once you learn and practice it becomes second nature. You end up replacing heavy cream or dairy milk for cashew milk in your coffee and staple cheeses for nutritional yeast. I cannot emphasize the importance of food education enough. It is what got me where I am today and I would highly suggest that you talk to a friend or family member about creating a weekly "Love Food" group! You can talk about food—not in an obsessive way—and further educate yourself about the food you eat, are afraid of or avoid due to societal norms.

Speaking of norms, this book is far from normal. It follows my journey and leads you through my darkest times. We eventually end up in a happy place but not without showing you the bumps involved in finding the light beyond the darkness. I want to encourage all of you to follow these recipes but not feel restricted or tied to the norms surrounding food and restriction. Do what you know works for you, suits the palate of your family and the needs of *you*—the most important person. This book will help you see that with some practice, self-love and belief that anything can happen. After all, ten years ago I was on my knees being sick in a toilet, crying about food and now I am writing a book on what used to be my worst enemy. Anything is possible if you just believe you deserve change.

I thought I couldn't do it but then I remembered the waking hell I lived through to be able to tell this story—at the time I had no idea it would end up in a book, in your hands.

I hope this cookbook will inspire you to eat food you thought was not good for you and help you see how beautiful you really are. These are the recipes I ate throughout my journey and they all have a really special place in my heart. With them, you will feel amazing, start seeing food more positively and eventually realize you are not alone. Everyone, in one way or another, has been afraid of food before and this book is here to help you fight that in every way possible. It will challenge you, make you cry and educate you. My goal is to leave you inspired and appreciating that, in fact, food is your friend.

Carby, Hearty and Comforting Mains

If you feel like taking a personal day and feeling sorry for yourself (we all do it, no shame, baby) then these recipes are for you! I used to fear food with every bone in my body but I remember when I was having a bad day all I wished I could eat was something hearty, carby and thick! I would sit in front of the refrigerator wishing I could have a piece of toast or bowl of spaghetti, whip up a burger or even order in pizza. I never understood that carbs were fuel or a form of energy; instead, I thought they were the highway to fat thighs, a flabby stomach and a fat ass. Can you believe that since then, I have thick thighs, love my stomach, have a big booty and EVEN EAT ALL THE CARBS? It took many years of education and food-eating practice but I no longer have uncertainties when it comes to foods like pizzas, burgers and pastas. I know these recipes will help you see that with a few tweaks and tricks you too can achieve the kitchen and body confidence you've always deserved!

Mushroom & White Truffle Oil Risotto with Vegan Cheese

SERVINGS: 4

This is comfort food at its finest but with a Maria untraditional twist—after all, I am not Italian, nor am I a risotto expert! This dish is extremely decadent from the richness of the truffle oil to the silkiness of the beautiful mushrooms. I love making this at home for Andrew and myself when it is super cold outside and we're hungry for something that reminds us of the peaceful cabins in the mountains.

When I am feeling guilty or unsure about a certain meal I try to remember the happy memories certain foods bring me. Sure, eating carbs isn't grade A healthy but for me I think it's important. Keeping myself happy keeps my mind at ease, which in turn helps me maintain the healthy relationship I've developed with my body!

4–6 cups (1–1.5 L) vegetable stock, unsalted

2 tbsp (30 ml) extra virgin olive oil

1 small yellow onion, finely chopped

2 cloves garlic, finely chopped

4 cups (384 g) assorted mushrooms, diced small (I use cremini and shiitake)

1 cup (190 g) arborio rice

¼ cup (60 ml) full-fat coconut cream

2 tbsp (30 ml) lemon juice

1 tsp white truffle oil

2 cups (60 g) fresh spinach, whole

Salt and pepper to taste

Chives

Fresh thyme

Lemon wedges

Vegan Parmesan cheese (page 187)

In a saucepan or pot over high heat, add the vegetable stock. Bring the stock to a boil, then reduce the heat to low and simmer.

In a medium-sized pot over medium heat, add the olive oil and heat it up for about 1 minute. Add the onion and garlic and cook for about 5 minutes or until they are translucent and golden brown. I like to use a wooden spoon to stir them occasionally while they brown. When the onions and garlic are brown, add in the mushrooms and cook them for 2 to 3 minutes. You want a golden color to develop, but you also want some depth to them otherwise they will just disappear during the cooking process.

Add the rice to the pot and give it a good stir. Using a ladle, add 1 cup (240 ml) of the warm vegetable stock to the pot and stir until the liquid is absorbed by the rice. Repeat this step until the rice is cooked. I like my risotto ultra-creamy so I make sure to stir throughout this whole process.

Just before serving, add the coconut cream, lemon juice, truffle oil, spinach and seasoning. Stir until the spinach has wilted, then serve with fresh chives, thyme, lemon wedges and vegan Parmesan cheese!

Did You Know?

"Real" truffle oil—yes not all truffle oil is real, so pay attention when purchasing—is extremely high in antioxidants? It is also a neat source of magnesium, zinc and iron!

A taste of thanksgiving Meatballs
SERVINGS: 4–6

There is really just something to be said about eating a "meat" ball but without the meat, and it still looking and tasting just as good as the "real" thing. I love eating this dish with pasta but feel free to swap that out and enjoy it with quinoa, barley or chickpeas. I also like to pair every dish with loads of greens, like salads or steamed vegetables, so enjoy this alongside a gorgeous green salad, green beans or broccoli. I find that if I pair my heavier pasta dishes with light, airy salads, my mind finds a comfortable safe space in that meal and I don't freak out about the fact that I am eating a nutrient-dense dish that society has made out to seem like the enemy.

NO-BEEF BASE

1 cup (25 g) cremini mushrooms, dehydrated

2 tsp (5 g) onion powder

2 tbsp (34 g) sea salt

1 tbsp (15 ml) olive oil

1 tbsp (2 g) dried sage

1 tbsp (2 g) parsley

1 tbsp (2 g) basil

1 tbsp (2 g) celery seasoning

1 tbsp (13 g) brown sugar

1 tsp garlic powder

1 tsp dill

1 tsp nutmeg

1 tsp paprika

1 tsp liquid smoke

1 tsp thyme

1 tsp coriander

Dash of Worcestershire (there are vegan brands on the market; I use Wizard)

"MEATBALLS"

2 tbsp (30 ml) extra virgin olive oil + more for cooking

¼ cup (37 g) small sweet onion, chopped

3 cloves of garlic, roughly chopped

2 tbsp (35 g) no-beef base

1 cup (84 g) rolled oats, divided

1½ cups (228 g) white kidney beans, drained

½ cup (30 g) fresh cilantro

½ cup (50 g) walnuts

Juice of ½ a lemon

SAUCE

2 tbsp (30 ml) extra virgin olive oil

1 small yellow onion, finely chopped

2 cloves garlic

2 cups (192 g) cremini mushrooms, roughly chopped

½ cup (120 ml) red wine

3 cups (720 ml) coconut cream or almond milk (if you prefer a lighter consistency)

2 tbsp (36 g) nutritional yeast

2 tbsp (16 g) arrowroot powder

1 tsp white wine vinegar

Salt and pepper to taste

Fresh parsley

Crushed walnuts

Lemon zest

(continued)

A TASTE OF THANKSGIVING MEATBALLS (CONTINUED)

The no-beef base is optional, but highly recommended as this stuff is amazing! It's perfect for soups, stews, potpies, meatloaves and more. Note that you must use dehydrated mushrooms; fresh won't work! Place all the base ingredients in a food processor and blend until well-combined. Put in a jar and store in the refrigerator for future meals. This base will last you a few months in the refrigerator, in a tightly sealed container.

For the meatballs, in a cast-iron skillet or frying pan over medium heat, warm the olive oil for 30 seconds. Lower the heat and add the onion, garlic and no-beef base and sauté until translucent and slightly golden. While the onions are cooking, add ½ cup (42 g) of oats to a food processor and pulse until they develop a flour-like consistency. Then add the beans, cilantro, walnuts, lemon juice and the onion mixture (excluding the remaining ½ cup [42 g] of oats), and blend until the mixture is well-combined. Transfer the mixture to a bowl and add the remaining ½ cup (42 g) of oats and stir until well-combined. Using a spoon, create tiny "meatballs," making sure to roll them really nice and tight, so they stay in good form! You should have about 24 meatballs. Cook them in the pan you previously used to cook the onions, using as much oil as you desire (I use around 3 tablespoons [45 ml]). Cook the meatballs over medium heat for 5 minutes on each side until golden brown, then put a lid on, turn it to low and give it a shake every couple of minutes.

For the sauce, sauté the olive oil, onion and garlic in the same way you did previously for the meatballs, on medium-to-low heat, until translucent and slightly golden. Add the mushrooms and let them cook down for at least 10 minutes. When your mushroom and onion mixture has reduced by half or more, add the red wine. Increase the heat to medium-high and cook down, without a lid, until all of the liquid has absorbed. When the liquid has absorbed into the mushroom mixture, add the coconut cream or almond milk and reduce heat to low. Add the nutritional yeast, arrowroot powder, vinegar and salt and pepper, stirring constantly until you notice a thicker consistency developing. The longer you cook down the arrowroot, the less you will be able to taste it in the sauce. Add the sauce to a blender (I use my Vitamix), and blend until completely smooth and creamy.

Add the sauce to the pan with the meatballs and stir until hot throughout. Garnish with parsley, walnuts and lemon zest. Enjoy immediately and be prepared to fight for these bad boys!

Did You Know?

Beans are well known for their role in finding a balanced, healthy weight. One reason for this is they contain inhibitors that stop the body from absorbing carbohydrates quickly and prevent blood-sugar spikes.

Greek-Style Jackfruit Gyros with Vegan Tzatziki and "Fries"

SERVINGS: 4

Ya'll didn't think I was going to write this cookbook and not include some sort of Greek gyros memoir, did you? I hope not because gyros are probably one of the most memorable and special recipes that my family would enjoy every summer back in Greece. We would line up behind tons of people and wait patiently on the streets of Astros at the shop where they prepared all our food. Traditionally gyros are made with pork, tzatziki, fresh veggies and even crispy French fries. I realize this recipe is far from traditional, so I hope my Greek folks will forgive me, but I think you'll enjoy these just as much or perhaps more.

There is nothing more special than being able to bring memories back into your own home in the form of food. I infused today's food trends and my own preferences into this dish to make it as fabulous as possible. I know you'll love it!

FRIES

3–4 medium-sized potatoes, cut into French fries

¼ cup (60 ml) extra virgin olive oil

½ cup (120 ml) lemon juice

3 cloves garlic, pressed

1 tsp oregano

Salt and pepper to taste

1 tbsp (15 ml) extra virgin olive oil

1 tsp cumin powder

1 tsp fresh jalapeño (optional), chopped (discard seeds)

Pinch of cloves and cinnamon

Splash of red wine vinegar

Juice of ½ a lemon

Salt and pepper to taste

JACKFRUIT PULLED PORK

2¼ cups (400 g) jackfruit, drained, with rough corners cut off

¼ cup (23 g) green pepper, very finely sliced

2 tbsp (4 g) fresh mint, finely chopped

3 cloves garlic, crushed

2 tsp (11 g) tomato paste

1 tbsp (3 g) dried oregano

1 tbsp (7 g) onion powder

PICKLED ONION

1 large red onion, thinly sliced

1 cup (240 ml) red wine vinegar

¼ cup (15 g) fresh parsley, roughly chopped

¼ cup (15 g) fresh mint, roughly chopped

1 tbsp (3 g) dried oregano

1 tsp salt

Juice of 1 lemon

(continued)

GREEK-STYLE JACKFRUIT GYROS
WITH VEGAN TZATZIKI AND "FRIES" (CONTINUED)

EXTRAS FOR SERVING

Pita bread

Vegan Tzatziki (see page 192)

Cherry tomatoes, halved

Cucumber, sliced widthwise

Lettuce, cut into bite-sized pieces

Fresh mint, whole

Dill leaves, stemmed and roughly chopped

Preheat the oven to 375°F (190°C) and line a baking sheet with parchment paper.

Put the potatoes, olive oil, lemon juice, garlic, oregano and salt and pepper in a large bowl and stir really well. If you really want things to be out of this world you could marinate this mixture for an hour before baking but if you're in a hurry just stir. Transfer to the baking sheet and cook for 35 minutes or until golden brown on the outside and steamy on the inside.

While the potatoes cook, put the jackfruit, green pepper, mint, garlic, tomato paste, oregano, onion powder, olive oil, cumin, jalapeño, cloves, cinnamon, vinegar, lemon juice and salt and pepper in a medium bowl. Combine the ingredients until the jackfruit is completely coated. Transfer the mixture to a nonstick frying pan and cook on medium heat for 15 to 20 minutes, using the back of your spatula to press down on the jackfruit as it cooks.

While the jackfruit cooks, prepare the pickled onions. Put the onion, vinegar, parsley, mint, oregano, salt and lemon juice in a bowl and stir well. Let the mixture sit for 30 minutes to 2 hours—the longer you let it sit the better.

When you are just about ready to serve the dish, warm the pitas in the oven at low heat. Fill the pita however you wish (reference the photo to see how I enjoy mine). Either fold the pita into a wrap or fold and wrap in a piece of paper and tie with string. Enjoy!

Did You Know?

Jackfruits are basically a spa in a fruit! This interesting yet adaptable fruit is amazing for hair growth and skin health—it even helps reduce wrinkles. So, if you're tired and want a pick-me-up then this is your meal. Jackfruit is packed with vitamins and minerals—it is especially high in copper, a mineral vital for thyroid metabolism and hormone production. It is also high in protein and a great source of energy!

"I'd Rather Be in Mexico" Vegan Tacos

SERVINGS: 6

When I was a teen the only way I would eat tacos was if they were slathered in a guacamole, sour cream and some sort of citrusy salad. Safe to say my palate has shifted quite a bit and I now turn to cashew cream for that heavy topping and lentils and red cabbage salad for taco fillings.

Green French lentils may seem like a weird addition to the taco family but I promise you, it works. They're really easy to make, fun for the family and they allow you to pick and choose what you want in your meal. Throughout my bulimia journey I would sometimes find myself feeling pressured into eating foods when there were no other options. Foods like tacos, salad bars and big Greek feasts really helped me ease into the idea of eating what I wanted and making the right choices for my body based on what I was craving, or how I was feeling that day!

TACO "MEAT"

2 cups (396 g) cooked green French lentils (or yellow lentils)

1 tbsp (15 ml) extra virgin olive oil

2 bay leaves

1 veggie stock cube

1 tbsp (15 ml) maple syrup

1 tsp garlic powder

1 tsp onion powder

½ tsp paprika

¼ tsp cinnamon

Juice of one lime

Salt and pepper to taste

PICKLED CABBAGE SALAD

2–3 cups (180–270 g) red cabbage, very thinly sliced

2 tsp salt, divided

3 tbsp (30 g) shallots, finely chopped

2 tbsp (30 ml) maple syrup

¼ tsp ginger

Juice of 2 limes

CILANTRO CASHEW CREAM

½ cup (70 g) cashews, raw, cover with water and soak overnight in the refrigerator

1 cup (60 g) fresh cilantro

¾ cup (180 ml) water

2 cloves garlic

Salt and pepper to taste

Juice of 1 lime

CRISPY CORN

1½ cups (250 g) corn

Salt and pepper to taste

PERFECT TACO TOPPINGS

Pico de gallo (see page 110)

Fresh avocado

Fresh cilantro

Your choice of tortilla

Green onions

Hot sauce of choice

(continued)

"I'D RATHER BE IN MEXICO" VEGAN TACOS (CONTINUED)

The taco "meat" is best if you make it the night before you plan to use it. To make it, cook the lentils, olive oil, bay leaves, veggie stock cube, maple syrup, garlic powder, onion powder, paprika, cinnamon, lime juice and salt and pepper over medium heat in a frying pan until crisp, around 10 to 12 minutes. Remove bay leaves. If you are making it ahead, store the cooked taco "meat" in the refrigerator. At the same time, you can soak the cashews in the refrigerator overnight.

For the pickled cabbage salad, put the cabbage in a large bowl with 4 cups (1 L) of water and 1 teaspoon of salt. Let this combination sit for 30 minutes. While the cabbage is soaking, place the shallots, maple syrup, 1 teaspoon of salt, ginger and lime juice in a high-speed blender and blend until smooth. When the cabbage is finished soaking, drain it and add the cabbage back to the bowl. Pour the dressing over the cabbage and mix well with your hands.

For the cashew cream, strain the cashews you soaked overnight in the refrigerator.

Put the drained cashews in a high-speed blender along with the cilantro, water, garlic, salt and pepper and lime juice and blend for 2 minutes. To serve the cashew cream, you can either dollop it out from a bowl or transfer the mixture into a sauce bottle.

To make the crispy corn, add the corn to a skillet and toast over medium heat, shaking for around 15 minutes, until crispy and season with salt and pepper to taste.

Serving the tacos is as simple as grabbing a taco shell; use whatever kind you prefer, it can be whole wheat, corn, homemade—it is your choice! Begin by adding the lentils, topping with the beautiful cabbage salad, fresh pico and your favorite garnishes. Dress the taco with the cashew cream.

Did You Know?

Fun fact: Canada is the world's largest producer of lentils! Lentils have an incredibly impressive nutrition profile and it's no surprise they are a staple food in cultures around the world. With almost 19 grams of protein per serving, lentils can help curb hunger sustainably and aid the body in daily muscle repair.

Lentil Burgers with Italian Bread Crumbs

These burgers have a lot going on but these babies pack a punch and are so much fun to make! Inspired by my Italian neighbors, this dish has a hint of the Mediterranean. My favorite part from this recipe is the fragrant parsley salad that you add as a topping.

Burgers don't always have to be bad for you and this recipe is the perfect example of why. These are made using hearty lentils, versatile brown rice and fully loaded sourdough bread crumbs. What I try to do when I am worried about eating something complex like a burger, pizza or sandwich is to mentally dissect each ingredient on my plate—here, you're basically eating a big-ass feast with a perfect balance of carbs, proteins, veggies and fats. There is nothing wrong with eating burgers and you better get used to that!

You can choose any toppings you like—some of my favorites are listed below. You can also choose to eat with or without a bun. Lettuce wraps are fun here too!

¼ cup + 1 tbsp (45 g) white onion, roughly chopped; squeeze out excess liquid

2 cloves garlic

2 tbsp (30 ml) extra virgin olive oil

1 cup (84 g) rolled oats

1 tsp garlic powder

1 tsp onion powder

1 tsp thyme

1 tsp oregano

1 tsp rosemary, roughly chopped

½ tsp paprika

Salt and pepper to taste

½ cup (85 g) sweet corn, fresh or from a can (drained)

1 cup (198 g) cooked yellow lentils (drained)

½ cup (30 g) fresh cilantro

1¼ cups (245 g) cooked brown rice, divided

1¼ cups (105 g) pulsed oats

⅛ tsp chili flakes

1 tbsp (6 g) flour of choice, I use chickpea

TOPPINGS

Fresh basil

Fresh spinach

Fresh tomato

Parsley salad (1 cup [60 g] parsley, roughly chopped, with olive oil, lemon, salt and pepper)

Vegan cheddar or mozzarella

Vegan mayo

Whole-wheat burger buns

(continued)

LENTIL BURGERS WITH ITALIAN BREAD CRUMBS (CONTINUED)

Preheat the oven to 375°F (190°C) and line a large baking sheet with parchment paper then spray with coconut oil or olive oil.

In a small cast-iron skillet over medium heat, sauté the olive oil, onion and garlic until translucent and golden.

While the onions cook, put the rolled oats, garlic powder, onion powder, thyme, oregano, rosemary, paprika and salt and pepper in a food processor and pulse just till well-combined, about 10 seconds. Then add corn, lentils, cilantro and 1 cup (195 g) of the cooked rice to the food processor and blend until smooth; the mixture should almost stick together. Transfer the mixture to a bowl. Add the oat crumbs, ¼ cup (50 g) cooked brown rice, the cooked onion mixture, chili flakes and flour. Stir till well-combined.

Let this mixture sit in the refrigerator for 30 minutes to an hour; letting the mixture sit helps it come together and become firm.

Using a ¼-cup mold, shape your patties. It helps to first add a bit of coconut oil and oat crumbs to the mold to avoid sticking. To release the patty, smack the mold down on a baking sheet. Then pat the patties down gently to flatten them for even cooking.

Bake the patties in the oven for 35 minutes, flipping them about halfway through. They should be nice and golden brown.

While the patties bake, prepare all your fixings, toast your buns and make your parsley salad.

Here's a tip: If you add your sauce to the bottom bun then the rest is a free-for-all! ENJOY!

Did You Know?

Parsley is packed full of chlorophyll, which helps build red blood cells and collagen. It also boosts your energy, is full of vitamin K and helps with your overall well-being! Parsley is also known for its diuretic properties, which helps with inflammation and relieves congestion in the kidneys— cool, right?

Skip the Dishes One-Pot Mushroom Spaghetti

SERVINGS: 4

One-pot pasta is new to me and my kitchen but it has quickly become a beloved dish in my household. Hands down this is one of the simplest ways to prepare pasta and still yield that creamy, beautiful sauce you would normally achieve, but without the extra hassle and dirty pots and pans! The possibilities don't end with pasta. I have made this dish in several different variations, with grains like farro, or even using orzo or rice. Really, it's as easy as adding your favorite ingredients, adding a stock or water, bringing it to a boil and waiting patiently. This dish is especially awesome because it's fortified with B12 from the nutritional yeast. If you're not on board with the nutritional yeast train yet, don't worry you still have time. Nutritional yeast has completely replaced Parmesan cheese in our household along with other staple dairy "must-haves."

I have so many memories—not always good ones—of eating pasta as a child and thinking to myself: "This will probably make me fat and I won't skate as well." As depressing and sad as those memories are, I am happy I found one-pot pasta and that it allowed me to see that everything in moderation is the best kind of happy to be! This recipe will actually make you happier, too. One pot, less mess, more time for wine and Netflix!

14 oz (400 g) spaghetti

2 cups (192 g) cremini mushrooms, chopped widthwise, with stem

1 large yellow onion, finely chopped

1 cup (180 g) fresh tomatoes, roughly chopped

½ cup (30 g) cilantro, fresh, finely chopped

3 tbsp (54 g) nutritional yeast

3 cloves garlic, pressed

1 tbsp (10 g) paprika

1 tbsp (10 g) coriander

Dash of chili flakes, or more to your liking

Salt and pepper to taste

4–6 cups (1–1.5 L) water

7 oz (200 ml) light coconut milk

Put the spaghetti, mushrooms, onion, tomatoes, cilantro, nutritional yeast, garlic, paprika, coriander, chili flakes, salt and pepper and 4 cups (1 L) of water in a deep pot. Bring to a boil then lower the heat and cook for about 30 minutes on medium heat with the lid on. As the pasta cooks keep an eye on it, and gradually add extra water to avoid burning. When your pasta reaches just before al dente add the coconut milk and cook for 5 minutes. Stir a lot at this point to make the pasta super creamy! That's it—you can thank me later!

the Perfect Pesto Pasta Dinner
SERVINGS: 4–5

What I love most about this dish is that everyone I have ever fed it to has fallen in love. It's moderately easy to make when having guests over, to take to a dinner party or even if you're just enjoying it on your own! In the summer of 2017 I made this dish with my mom and she's always been a skeptic about meals that don't have dairy or meat, so you can say she wasn't anticipating a winner from this dish. I snuck away from the kitchen while the pasta was cooking to use the washroom and when I returned I caught my mom snatching a slurp of my fabulous pesto. Before she knew I was in the kitchen I overheard her whisper, "Shit, that's good." Safe to say this is a big hit with the family and I think I somehow managed to convince them to use dairy substitutes when making their next pasta dish. P.S. Don't be afraid to try this dish with ingredients like sundried tomatoes, fresh olives or even capers!

1 lb (450 g) spaghetti

1 small head broccoli, cut into small florets

2 cups (50 g) fresh basil

½ cup (50 g) walnuts

¼ cup (60 ml) extra virgin olive oil

¼–½ cup (60-120 ml) warm water

Juice of one lemon

3 tbsp (54 g) nutritional yeast

2 garlic cloves

½ tsp red pepper flakes

Salt and pepper to taste

1 cup (150 g) cherry tomatoes, halved

1 cup (30 g) fresh spinach

½ cup (70 g) Kalamata olives, halved and whole

¼ cup (16 g) seeds of choice (I used pumpkin and sunflower)

Sprinkling of red pepper flakes

Cook the spaghetti in salted, boiling water according to package directions. Five minutes before the pasta has finished cooking, add the broccoli to the pot and cook until tender. Drain the pasta and broccoli.

While the pasta is cooking, put the basil, walnuts, olive oil, ¼ cup (60 ml) of warm water, lemon juice, nutritional yeast, garlic, red pepper flakes and salt and pepper in a food processor and blend until smooth. You can slowly add more warm water for a smoother pesto. If you'd like to get technical you can add everything but the olive oil and slowly add the oil as you blend for an extra creamy effect.

Put the pasta and broccoli in a large mixing bowl, add the pesto and give it a good toss until everything is well-coated. Just before serving, add beautiful toppings like tomatoes, spinach, olives, seeds and red pepper flakes!

Enjoy hot or cold.

In the Kitchen tip

To keep your basil bright in sauces, blanch the leaves for 5 seconds in boiling water to kill the browning enzymes. Transfer to ice water for a quick "shock," pat dry with a paper towel and continue with the recipe.

Roasted Red Pepper Rigatoni Cake SERVINGS: 5–6

That's right. You read it properly so sit down and get comfortable with the recipe because you're about to make a bad-ass rigatoni cake and wow the whole world with your stellar kitchen skills. This red-pepper sauce is hands down one of the best sauces I have ever made. There's a certain sexiness about it—maybe because it's made from nourishing ingredients and it makes me feel goddess AF while eating it? Anyway, I'll let you all be the judges but let me just remind you that this sauce can be eaten on anything and everything. Last night's rice leftovers, those lentil balls in the refrigerator, or even spread on your favorite pizza dough recipe!

2 tbsp (30 ml) extra virgin olive oil, divided

1 lb (450 g) rigatoni

2 roasted red peppers

1 cup (180 g) fresh tomatoes

1 cup (140 g) cashews

Juice of 1–2 lemons (I love lemon!)

2 tbsp (36 g) nutritional yeast

1 tbsp (2 g) coriander flakes

¼ cup (60 ml) warm water

1 tbsp (10 g) garlic powder

Salt and pepper to taste

1 cup (288 g) vegan cream cheese (I used a cashew-based one)

1–2 cups (150–300 g) cherry tomatoes, halved

1 cup (115 g) vegan mozzarella

½ cup (30 g) fresh flat-leaf parsley, finely chopped

Preheat the oven to 400°F (200°C) and grease a 9-inch (23-cm) springform pan with 1 tablespoon (15 ml) of olive oil.

Cook the rigatoni in boiling, salted water for a few minutes less than instructed on the package. Drain the pasta and toss with 1 tablespoon (15 ml) of olive oil to prevent it from sticking. Set aside.

For the sauce, add the roasted peppers, tomatoes, cashews, lemon juice, nutritional yeast, coriander, warm water, garlic powder and salt and pepper to a high-speed blender. Blend until smooth, transfer the sauce to a bowl and set aside.

To assemble the cake, put about one third of the sauce in the bottom of the springform pan and spread it around evenly. Then, stand each piece of cooked rigatoni on its end in the pan. Continue until the whole pan is tightly packed with the rigatoni. Spread the vegan cream cheese over the top, using a spoon to get an even coating. Pour the remainder of the sauce over the top and spread thoroughly. Use your fingers or the end of a spoon to get sauce into each pasta piece. Finish off with fresh cherry tomatoes—add as many or as few as you'd like, but I covered the top of the cake with them!

Bake for 15 minutes. Remove that deliciousness from the oven and top with the mozzarella cheese. Bake for another 15 minutes, then let stand for 10 minutes. Sprinkle with the chopped parsley.

Using a sharp knife, cut down along the sides of the pan to avoid sticking. Open the springform pan, cut into slices and enjoy!

Healthy Alfredo Sauce (It's Possible!)

As far as I'm concerned, alfredo sauce has gotten a bad rap for being processed, too creamy and overusing dairy, but it really doesn't have to! We live in 2018 and some of us know that cashews, almond milk and some nooch (nutritional yeast) whipped up in a blender will make some bad-ass sauce—and now you know it too! Fettuccine was one of the first dishes I cut out when I was going through the confusing stages of my teens and early twenties. Please, remember, I am a huge advocate for balance so don't cut the original version out of your diet because you think it's bad. You can eat what you want; I just made adjustments to the original recipe to help balance my life, my way. Andrew and I enjoy this healthy version of the dish almost three times a month and love every mouthful of it. I leave the table feeling energized, happy about my food choices and often ready to eat another serving.

1 lb (450 g) fettucine

2 tbsp (30 g) vegan butter

1 cup (140 g) raw cashews

1 medium yellow onion, finely sliced

3 cloves garlic

Salt and pepper to taste

½ cup (120 ml) white wine

Juice of 1 large lemon

½ tsp liquid smoke

1 tbsp (8 g) arrowroot powder

3 tbsp (54 g) nutritional yeast

½–1 cup (120–240 ml) almond milk

½ cup (120 ml) pasta water, and more for blending

¼ cup (15 g) fresh chives

¼ cup (15 g) fresh parsley

1 cup (150 g) fresh cherry tomatoes, halved, optional

½ cup (45 g) coconut bacon (page 80), optional

1 cup (252 g) smoked tofu cubes, optional

Cook the fettucine in boiling salted water according to package directions. Drain, saving ½ cup (120 ml) or more of the pasta water.

Heat the vegan butter in a large saucepan over medium heat. Let it melt, and then add the cashews, onion and garlic. Let this cook down for about 10 minutes on medium heat until the onions are translucent and the room is very fragrant. Add salt and pepper, then increase the heat and add the white wine and lemon to deglaze the pan. Using a silicone spoon, stir the mixture well, making sure to get all that goodness from the bottom of the pan. Cook until the wine has evaporated. Add the liquid smoke, arrowroot and nutritional yeast. Stir until well-combined.

Transfer this mixture to a high-speed blender, add the pasta water and almond milk, and blend for a minute or until completely smooth. If you need to loosen up the mixture add some more pasta water. Taste the sauce to make sure you cannot taste the arrowroot powder. If you can, stir for a while longer over low heat, tasting it occasionally. When you can't taste it any more, it's time to add the pasta. Give it a good stir and transfer to a large serving dish. Garnish with the fresh herbs. Best enjoyed hot with fresh garlic toast. If you want to add some extra flair, you can add fresh cherry tomatoes, coconut bacon or smoked tofu!

Cauliflower Greek Burgers

Your mouth has been invited to the best party ever with this vegan version of a burger. It's so simple to make using cauliflower, something I really don't cook with that often. While I was suffering with irritable bowel syndrome (IBS), cauliflower was one of my worst nightmares and would almost immediately trigger my symptoms. Luckily, I overcame those symptoms by continuing to eat what my body wanted to and learning how to treat the symptoms with healthy remedies like ginger tea; castor-oil rubs; and the wonder tablet, digestive enzymes! I know you'll love these burgers and they'll soon become a family favorite!

BURGERS

2 flax eggs (2 tbsp [30 g] ground flaxseeds and 6 tbsp [90 ml] hot water)

1½ cups (160 g) cauliflower, cut into florets

2 tbsp (30 ml) olive oil, divided

¼ cup + 1 tbsp (45 g) yellow onion, roughly chopped

3 cloves garlic, roughly chopped

1 tbsp (3 g) dill

2 tsp (2 g) oregano

1 tsp thyme

Dash of paprika

Dash of chili flakes

½ cup (50 g) walnuts

2 tbsp (30 ml) almond milk

¾ cup (150 g) cooked brown rice

Salt and pepper to taste

4 tbsp (24 g) chickpea flour

CASHEW CREAM (OPTIONAL FOR TOPPING)

1½ cups (210 g) raw cashews, soaked in hot water for 20 minutes or in cold water for at least 4 hours

Juice from 1 lemon

2 cloves garlic, pressed

1 tsp oregano

1 tsp olive oil

2 tbsp (36 g) nutritional yeast

2 tbsp (30 ml) water

Salt and pepper to taste

OLIVE SALSA

2 cups (300 g) heirloom tomatoes, diced, seeded

4 tbsp (60 ml) olive oil

⅓ cup (45 g) Kalamata olives, seeded, chopped

¼ cup (65 g) chopped fresh basil, finely chopped

3 large cloves garlic, minced

1 shallot, finely chopped

Salt and pepper to taste

2 tbsp (30 ml) lemon juice

(continued)

FIXINGS

Buns of choice

Fresh lettuce, tomatoes and basil

Vegan tzatziki (page 192)

Note

The cashew cream is optional, but recommended if you want to make the tzatziki. Use leftovers as a dip or spread.

Preheat the oven to 375°F (190°C), line a baking sheet with parchment paper and lightly grease with coconut oil or olive oil.

To prepare the flax eggs, add the hot water to the flax in a small bowl and let sit for 5 minutes (watch as it thickens similar to the consistency of an egg).

Cook the cauliflower florets in a frying pan or cast-iron skillet on high heat with 1 tablespoon (15 ml) of olive oil until toasty and golden. Stir often to avoid burning. You want the florets to look as though you roasted them. Remove the cauliflower from the pan and set aside. In the same pan, add the remaining tablespoon (15 ml) of olive oil, onion, garlic, dill, oregano, thyme, paprika and chili flakes. Sauté over medium heat until the onion is translucent and golden.

While the onion mixture is cooking, put the cauliflower, walnuts, almond milk and rice in a food processor and combine for about a minute, stopping to scrape the sides if necessary. Season to taste. Be careful not to overblend, creating a mashed potato consistency, which we don't want. Transfer this mixture to a bowl and stir in the chickpea flour, flax eggs and sautéed onion mixture. Let the mixture rest in the refrigerator for 30 minutes. Remove the mixture from the refrigerator and, using a greased, ½-cup scoop, roll each patty into a ball and then flatten to achieve a burger-like shape. Place the patties on the greased baking sheet and cook in the oven for 30 to 35 minutes, flipping halfway through. Use a paper towel to soak up the excess oil when you transfer the patties to a plate.

While the burgers are baking, to make the cashew cream, put the cashews, lemon juice, gralic, oregano, olive oil and nutritional yeast into a food processor and combine until smooth. Add water 1 tablespoon (15 ml) at a time and continue blending until you reach the best consistency. I achieved my preferred consistency with 2 tablespoons (30 ml) of water. This process could take up to 2 minutes; you may have to stop occasionally to check the consistency and scrape the sides of the food processor, adding the water as you see fit. Season to taste.

To prepare the olive salsa, put the tomatoes, olive oil, olives, basil, garlic, shallot, lemon juice and salt and pepper in a bowl and stir until well-combined. That's it!

Assemble the burgers by toasting the buns, slathering with cashew cream or tzatziki, adding a patty then topping with fresh tomatoes, basil, olive salsa and lettuce. Enjoy!

team Pizza! Simple Pizza Dough

PIZZA?! Hell to the no. There is no way I am going to eat pizza, it'll go straight to my stomach and I will regret it immediately. Those were my thoughts for 5 to 6 years straight. I didn't think I could eat anything that involved carbs, especially not pizza. Who gave pizza such a bad rep to begin with? We all eat toast in the morning, right? Or oats? Or a full-blown pasta meal (ok, maybe only some of us do this)? How is that any different from a few slices of bread with some beautiful toppings? It's all your choice and you can make pizza anything you want it to be. Feel free to break the rules while cooking in order to strengthen your relationship between food and your body in the kitchen!

1½ cups (360 ml) warm water

2 packets active dried yeast

4 cups (500 g) plain flour

2 tsp (12 g) salt

Dash of fresh cracked pepper

¼ cup (60 ml) extra virgin olive oil

Combine the water and active dry yeast in a bowl and set aside for 5 minutes until foam forms.

On a flat surface pile the flour, sprinkle with salt and pepper then make a well in the center of the flour. Slowly pour the water and yeast mixture into the well. Add the olive oil to the well and then gently mix the dry and wet ingredients, folding the flour into the middle slowly. This is the act of kneading. Knead for about 10 minutes until the dough is smooth and elastic.

Brush a bowl with oil and place the dough inside. Put a tea towel over the bowl and allow it to rise in a warm place for 30 minutes to 1 hour. The dough should double in size.

Divide the dough into three balls. Flour a surface and use a rolling pin (or a wine bottle if you don't have one!) to flatten out and shape the dough into a circle. The dough should be about an ⅛ to ¼ inch (3 to 6 mm) thick. Poke the dough all over with a fork to prevent air pockets and then top with your toppings. Bake for 12 minutes on a baking sheet, turning halfway through.

In the Kitchen tip

After your dough has risen, been divided and is ready to be rolled, you can wrap the dough balls in plastic wrap and freeze for up to 3 months! On the morning you plan to make pizza, grab a dough ball from the freezer and place in an oiled bowl covered with plastic wrap (or a wet towel) in the refrigerator until it is soft. Remove from the refrigerator and let it sit for 30 minutes.

When Greeks Marry Italians Pizza SERVINGS: 1 PIZZA

This pizza is the best of both worlds! Its has delicious flavor and texture, but is also filled with nutrients. I love making this pizza when I want something comforting but I still want it to be nourishing and light. This pizza will always win over your hearts!

1 ball Team Pizza! Simple Pizza Dough (page 43) or 8 oz (230 g) store-bought dough

3–4 tbsp (45–60 g) Pomodoro or tomato sauce

½ cup (58 g) vegan mozzarella

1¼ cups (200 g) yellow onion, finely chopped

1 clove garlic, pressed

¼ cup (35 g) Kalamata olives

2 tbsp (17 g) capers

¼ cup (38 g) cherry tomatoes, halved

1 tsp olive oil

Salt and pepper to taste

Sprinkle of nutritional yeast

½ cup (10 g) arugula

Preheat the oven to 525°F (275°C)—don't freak about the high heat—this will help the pizza be perfect, crunchy and cooked throughout! See note about pans below.

Using a rolling pin, roll out the dough to a thickness of an ⅛ to ¼ inch (3 to 6 mm) thick. Spread the sauce over the dough to within ½ inch (13 mm) of the edge to leave a crust. Top with mozzarella, onion, garlic, olives, capers and cherry tomatoes. Press a fork all the way around the crust, leaving an imprint, then brush with olive oil.

Bake for about 12 minutes, turning the baking sheet halfway through the cooking time. Keep an eye on the crust; you want it to be golden, not burnt! Before eating, sprinkle with salt, pepper, nutritional yeast and arugula.

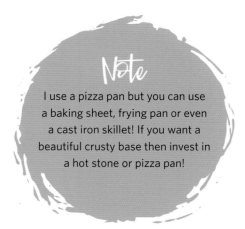

Note

I use a pizza pan but you can use a baking sheet, frying pan or even a cast iron skillet! If you want a beautiful crusty base then invest in a hot stone or pizza pan!

Cauliflower Buffalo Bites with Spinach and Capers Pizza

SERVINGS: 1 PIZZA

This pizza is inspired by the Stranger Wings Pizza at Virtuous Pie in Vancouver, Canada. I mean, come on! Can a buffalo chicken wing pizza be bad? I surely don't think so. It's creamy, crunchy and fabulous! I love the combination of spice and tang so much that I would suggest doubling the wings recipe and saving some to enjoy with your pizza (I know, I am extra).

BUFFALO BITES

½ cup (120 ml) almond milk

½ cup (46 g) chickpea flour, any flour works really!

3 cloves garlic, pressed

Salt and pepper to taste

1 tsp dill powder

½ head of cauliflower, chopped into small bite-sized pieces

½ cup (120 g) buffalo hot sauce

1 tsp extra virgin olive oil

PIZZA

1 ball Team Pizza! Simple Pizza Dough (page 43) or 8 oz (230 g) store-bought dough

3–4 tbsp (45–60 g) Pomodoro, or leftover hot sauce mixture from buffalo bites

1 cup (115 g) vegan mozzarella

½ cup (15 g) fresh spinach

2 tsp (6 g) capers

Preheat the oven to 450°F (230°C), line a baking sheet with parchment paper and set aside.

In a medium-sized bowl combine the almond milk, flour, garlic, salt and pepper and dill and stir till well-combined. Add the cauliflower and stir until well-coated. Using tongs, place the individual pieces of coated cauliflower onto the baking sheet and bake for 10 to 15 minutes or until golden and crisp.

While your cauliflower bakes, combine the hot sauce and oil in another medium-sized bowl and stir well.

Remove the cauliflower from the oven and bathe in this magical hot sauce until completely submerged and covered! Using tongs, remove the cauliflower pieces from the hot sauce and place back on a baking sheet and return to the oven. Bake for another 5 minutes, or until you can tell they have dried out a bit. Save any remaining hot sauce to use as pizza sauce if you would like, or save for another time.

Set aside the cauliflower and increase the oven heat to 525°F (275°C).

Using a rolling pin, roll out the dough to a thickness of ⅛ to ¼ inch (3 to 6 mm). Spread the sauce over the dough to within ½ inch (13 mm) of the edge to leave a crust. Top with mozzarella, cauliflower buffalo wings, spinach and capers. Be careful how much cauliflower you add as it may affect cooking time; I suggest about ½ cup (115 g). Press a fork all the way around the crust, leaving an imprint, then brush with olive oil.

Bake for about 12 minutes, turning the baking sheet halfway through. Keep an eye on the crust; you want it to be golden, not burnt! Now go enjoy this bomb as fuck pizza!

the Creamiest Mushroom Soup

SERVINGS: 4

I love mushrooms. Ok now that that's out in the open I will introduce you to this filling, creamy, satisfying and hearty soup—perfect for a cold fall or winter evening. You can make loads, refrigerate it and enjoy it throughout the week, but I have the feeling that won't be the case as this recipe often doesn't last the night in my house!

Soups are super fun because you can add so many nutrients to your pot without sacrificing flavor. As horrible as this may sound, I am going to say it anyway: soups are perfect for people who are suffering with eating disorders. Throw that shit in a cup and sip it down and pretend it's a luscious drink. If that's what it takes to keep a meal down and allow your mind to believe it's something it's not, then that's a good first step!

I love cooking down my onions, garlic and mushrooms until they are caramelized before adding the liquid into the pot. This method really ensures you have a fragrant and delicious dish in the making! Note that you don't have to use coconut milk; if you want a lighter, less rich soup you can also try almond or soy milk.

1 tbsp (15 ml) extra virgin olive oil

1 medium sweet onion, diced small

6 cloves garlic, pressed

5 cups (480 g) assorted mushroom, with stems, finely chopped (I use shiitake and cremini)

3 tbsp (7 g) fresh thyme (around 5 sprigs)

1 bay leaf

½ cup (120 ml) white wine

3 cups (720 ml) unsalted vegetable broth

1½ cups (360 ml) full-fat coconut milk (from a can)

1 tbsp (18 g) nutritional yeast

1 tbsp (8 g) arrowroot powder, mixed with 6 tbsp (90 ml) cold liquid (stock or water), whisked until smooth

Salt and pepper to taste

Fresh thyme

Green onion, finely chopped

Drizzle of oil

In a large soup pot heat the olive oil on high for 30 seconds. Add the onion, reduce the heat to medium and let it sweat for around 5 minutes or until golden brown. Add the garlic and cook for about 1 minute. Stir occasionally to avoid burning. Add the mushrooms, thyme and bay leaf and let the mixture cook down until reduced by half. Set aside a few cooked mushrooms for garnish. Increase the temperature to high and deglaze the pot with the white wine. Stir until all the bits from the bottom of the pot are loosened, then pour the broth, coconut milk and nutritional yeast into a pot and bring to a boil. Lower the heat and simmer on low for about 10 minutes. Then add in the arrowroot powder mixture and stir the soup with a whisk or spoon until well-combined. Cook for another 5 minutes on low heat. Season to taste with salt and pepper.

You can enjoy the soup thick and hearty or blend it for a smooth, beautiful silky effect—the choice is yours, and either decision will be amazing! I remove half of the soup from the pot, put it in a blender and whir it smooth, then add the blended soup back into the pot. You can also use an immersion blender and blend as much or as little as you would like.

Enjoy with the reserved mushrooms, fresh thyme, green onions and a light drizzling of olive oil!

Note

Sometimes a squeeze of lemon really brings out the flavor in this creamy, beautiful soup!

Hearty Vegetable Minestrone SERVINGS: 4–5

This soup brings me straight back to my childhood. It's super simple because all you need is one pot, just over ten ingredients and a bit of time to allow the flavors to simmer as you get on with your day! I recommend you enjoy a bowl of this minestrone soup with cheesy toast and fresh herbs.

Growing up we used to always go to the restaurant, Kabos, which my parents own in Swift Current, Saskatchewan, and enjoy a bowl of soup, do some child work (make coffee, clean tables for fun, fill waters). This place was and will forever be my second home: a place where I learned to socialize and to work my ass off, and it is where my love for food was first born. I am crying just typing this because it brings back so many memories. Weekends and Mondays were vegetable soup. Tuesday's soup was chicken noodle. Wednesday was lentil. Thursday was bean and bacon. Friday was traditional Greek avgolemono (otherwise known as lemon rice) soup. It's safe to say this recipe is really special to me and reminds me of the good old days.

2 tbsp (30 ml) extra virgin olive oil

1 sweet white onion, finely diced

3 cloves garlic

1 cup (100 g) celery stalk, finely chopped

1 cup (128 g) carrot, cubed

Handful of fresh thyme and oregano, chopped

2 cups (248 g) zucchini, cubed, 1 inch (2.5 cm) thick

1 cup (150 g) red pepper, cubed, 1 inch (2.5 cm) thick

2 cups (360 g) tomatoes, roughly chopped

2 cups (200 g) green beans, cut into 3-inch (8-cm) pieces

8 cups (2 L) unsalted vegetable stock

½ cup (100 g) orzo

Salt and pepper to taste

Squeeze of lemon

Fresh cilantro and parsley

In a large soup pot heat the olive oil on high for about 30 seconds. Lower the heat to medium and add the onion, garlic, celery and carrot and let them cook down for about 5 minutes. Stir occasionally to avoid burning. When the onions have become translucent, add the thyme and oregano. Give the mixture a gentle stir then add the remaining vegetables—zucchini, pepper, tomatoes and green beans. Cook the vegetables down for a few minutes on medium heat. Just as their color brightens, add the stock. Bring the mixture to a boil then simmer for 15 minutes. Add the orzo and cook for another 10 minutes. Taste test, and add salt and pepper if needed.

Enjoy immediately with a squeeze of lemon and more fresh herbs!

Did You Know?

Hot/warm foods help with digestion and bloating. When you learn to listen to your body and understand why you are craving certain foods you gain a stronger relationship with your body. In turn, your body will love you back for nourishing it so well!

My Travels in a Little Memory Bowl—Lime Coconut Curry Soup

SERVINGS: 4—5

This is going to be your go-to recipe when you're tight for time but quite hungry and want to enjoy an amazing meal! There is no real way to describe the flavors in this dish, but you will certainly experience an explosion of sweetness from the sweet potato, a tang from the gorgeous lime and a certain kick and flare from the exotic spices. All the elements in this soup are balanced and really leave you with a hero dish. This soup is inspired by my time in Thailand, where I learned to love myself, my body and the world around me. Oh, and where I met my British boyfriend of 5 years!

2 tbsp (14 g) coconut oil

1 tbsp (15 g) vegan butter

1 medium sweet onion, roughly chopped

1 green onion, roughly chopped

A few leaves fresh basil

½ tbsp (3 g) curry spice

½ tbsp (3 g) turmeric

½ tbsp (3 g) paprika

⅛ tsp cayenne pepper

Salt and pepper to taste

4 cups (600 g) sweet potato, cubed

6½ cups (1.5 L) unsalted vegetable stock

1 cup (240 ml) coconut milk

Juice of 1 large lime

Handful of fresh cilantro

Fresh lime juice

Lime zest

Toasted cashews

Fresh cilantro

In a large soup pot over high heat, warm the coconut oil and vegan butter for about 30 seconds. Add the onions and let them cook down on high heat for about 5 minutes. Stir occasionally to avoid burning. Add the basil, curry, turmeric, paprika and cayenne. Give the mixture a good stir then add the potatoes and let them cook on medium heat for about 5 minutes, or until a golden coating develops. Add the stock, bring to a boil, then simmer on low heat for about 20 minutes or until the potatoes are completely cooked through and tender. Add the coconut milk, lime juice and cilantro. Cook for another 3 to 5 minutes.

Depending on how courageous you are, you can blend the hot mixture immediately or you can let it cool a bit first then blend and reheat. You can use an immersion blender, or ladle the soup into a blender and blend to your desired texture. I love this soup silky smooth so I blend the whole pot. If you like your soups chunky then you can blend half for a heartier version. Enjoy topped with fresh lime juice and zest, cashews and cilantro—yum!

Did You Know?

Sweet potatoes are actually tubers, not potatoes. These bright orange beauties are loaded with beta-carotene, a compound that is converted into vitamin A in the body. Vitamin A improves the circulation of oxygen to hair follicles, which leads to a healthy scalp and stronger hair growth!

Back to My Roots

I can't possibly be sharing my favorite Greek recipes with you all! Or am I?
This is crazy and I am so excited for you to try what I loved to eat growing up
and the recipes that remind me most of my grandmothers and the summers
spent in Greece. These recipes are all very comforting to me. They are more
time-consuming than the last and they require a dash more love and patience
but once they're put together I assure you, you'll be hooked. The meals you
seek from traditional Greek restaurants can be made in the pots and stoves in
your own home. Filled with dense nutrients, crispness and culture, you'll be left
satisfied and happy! Hell, maybe your household might even end up louder,
more aggressive and honest—I think that's what happened to my family?

These recipes are perfect for family gatherings or intimate dates but especially
if you're looking to WOW your in-laws or parents!

Rice & Dill Stuffed Grape Leaves (DOLMADES) SERVINGS: 4–5

Oh baby, welcome to flavor town. These are about to blow your mind and leave your family and friends excited to come back around for dinner. I realize they are a bit more work than most of my recipes but you can't mess with tradition, folks, so just be patient and trust that these taste like love in your mouth when you're finished.

The combination of lemon, dill and silky rice is perfect and the tastes complement each other well. I highly recommend trying the vegan lemon sauce but please note that this recipe is traditionally made using eggs, so if you want to stick to tradition then call your nearest Greek grandma and snatch that recipe off her!

30 grape leaves

1 yellow onion, finely chopped in a food processor

4 green onion stems, finely chopped

1 cup (9 g) fresh dill, finely chopped, stems removed (can also add parsley), plus more for garnish

7 tbsp (105 ml) extra virgin olive oil, divided

1 cup (185 g) white rice

Salt and pepper to taste

4 slices lemon, ½-inch (13-mm) thick

Vegetable stock, enough to cover dolmades in the pot

1 tbsp (8 g) cornstarch

½ cup (120 ml) lemon juice

Lemon wedges

Add enough water to halfway fill a medium-sized pot. Add the grape leaves to the water and bring to a boil then reduce the heat to low and simmer for about 30 minutes or until tender to touch.

While the grape leaves are cooking, put the yellow onion and green onion stems in a food processor and pulse for about 30 seconds; you do not want them to be very finely chopped, just well-blended. Remove from the processor and set aside. Add the dill to the food processor and process for about 20 seconds or until very finely chopped. If you do not want to use a food processor you can cut it by hand.

When the grape leaves are cooked, drain them and lay them in a bowl or on a plate nice and flat so they will be easy to roll later. Check for large stems at the base of the leaf; if they are long just give them a little chop.

In the same pot you used for the grape leaves, warm 4 tablespoons (60 ml) of olive oil and the onion and cook over medium heat until the onions are soft. You will know when they're ready when your home begins to smell very fragrant.

In a large mixing bowl put the rice, dill and onions mixture. Stir well and season with salt and pepper. Let this mixture sit for 10 to 15 minutes.

In a medium-sized pot put a few grape leaves and the lemon slices.

(continued)

RICE & DILL STUFFED GRAPE LEAVES (DOLMADES) (CONTINUED)

Now it is time to begin assembling our little beauties! Start by holding a grape leaf, stem side up, in your palm. Scoop about a tablespoon full of the rice mixture onto the leaf. Close the leaf by folding over the top and then the two sides. Finally, tuck it in all tight with the bottom. Place the dolmades in the pot and make sure that they're very close together to ensure they don't fall apart while cooking. Repeat this step until you've used up all the grape leaves. Drizzle the remainder of the olive oil (3 tablespoons [45 ml]) over the rolled dolmades. Add enough vegetable stock to just cover the dolmades then place a small plate on top (you want the plate to touch the dolmades). Bring to a boil then lower the heat and simmer for about 1 hour, or until the rice is cooked. Reserve 1 cup (240 ml) of juice from the pot to make the lemon sauce. If there is not enough juice to equal 1 cup (240 ml), add some hot water.

To make the lemon sauce, put the cornstarch in a bowl, then add 1 cup (240 ml) of juice from your pot and stir until well-combined. Slowly add the lemon juice to the mixture and beat like you would an egg. Pour the sauce into a pot, heat on high for a minute until the sauce thickens, and then serve, poured over the dolmades. Sprinkle with the dill and serve with some lemon wedges for squeezing over the dolmades.

Did You Know?

Grape leaves are used in traditional herbal medicine to combat a variety of ailments including heavy menstrual bleeding, canker sores and stomach aches.

Notes

You can find grape leaves in the ethnic section of many grocery stores; they are most commonly sold jarred or canned. If some leaves are larger than others, add more rice mixture accordingly. You could add up to an extra teaspoon when they're a bit larger. At first, your grape leaves will not seem so tender but as the dish sits they begin to tenderize! Sometimes, these are best enjoyed as leftovers and heated before consuming!

Spinach Pies (SPANAKOPITA) SERVINGS: 24

I am a huge sucker for spanakopita (or anything wrapped in phyllo pastry, for that matter)! Spanakopita are super addicting because they are crunchy, buttery and perfect. Every Greek event, party, wedding or baptism I've ever been to has had spanakopita and this dish is almost always the star of the show. I remember when I was little I would fight for these with my sister and my brother. We were only allowed to eat five before dinner because mom knew we wouldn't eat our main meal if we had too many—and it's almost impossible to just eat five!

Honestly, if there were a Greek food bible, this recipe would be the first in the book! These are traditionally enjoyed with tzatziki and feta cheese. You can try my Vegan tzatziki on page 192.

1 (16-oz [454-g]) package vegan phyllo pastry, thawed

½ cup (120 ml) extra virgin olive oil, divided

2 cups (320 g) yellow onion, finely chopped

1 cup (70 g) green onion, finely chopped

1½ cups (15 g) fresh dill, finely chopped, discard stems

Salt and pepper to taste

1 tbsp (18 g) nutritional yeast

1 vegetable stock cube

12–13 cups (400 g) spinach, fresh, whole

3 tbsp (27 g) white sesame seeds

The night before making your spanakopita remove the phyllo pastry from the freezer. Let it thaw in the refrigerator.

Into a large pot, heat 4 tablespoons (60 ml) of olive oil over medium heat for about 30 seconds, then add the yellow onions and sauté for about 10 minutes, until caramelized and golden brown. Stir often to avoid burning. Add the green onions, dill, salt, pepper, nutritional yeast and vegetable stock cube. Cook for about 2 minutes or until everything is wilted considerably. Add the spinach and stir until wilted and there is no moisture left. When the spinach is ready, remove from the heat and let cool for about 10 minutes.

While the spinach mixture is cooling, you can prep the phyllo. Have ¼ cup (60 ml) of olive oil and a pastry brush ready. It is easiest to work with phyllo when it is cool and moist, so keep the sheets as cool as possible. To keep the pastry moist, you can cover it with a damp cloth or use a spray bottle to occasionally spray the phyllo. All it needs is a touch, one spray each time with do!

(continued)

Note
You may not use the entire package of phyllo dough; put the rest back in the freezer for another use.

SPINACH PIES (SPANAKOPITA) (CONTINUED)

Gently place one sheet of phyllo on a cutting board. This is a very delicate ingredient, so be patient. Brush the whole sheet with olive oil, place another sheet on top and brush it with oil. Repeat these steps until you have a total of six sheets in your pile. Using a very sharp knife cut through the phyllo lengthwise three times (to make four rectangles). Scoop a heaped teaspoon of the spinach mixture onto one end of each strip of phyllo, leaving a little room around the edges. Fold the bottom right corner of each strip of phyllo up to meet with the opposite top corner and continue folding until you have little triangles of spinach pie! Each triangle should be as compact as can be.

Repeat these steps till you have 24 spanakopita. Sprinkle each little spanakopita with some sesame seeds. Place the spanakopita onto a plate and store in the freezer for 30 minutes. While the spanakopita are in the freezer, preheat the oven to 400°F (205°C).

Place the spanakopita on a baking sheet and brush with olive oil one more time. Bake for 20 minutes or until golden brown and perfectly crispy!

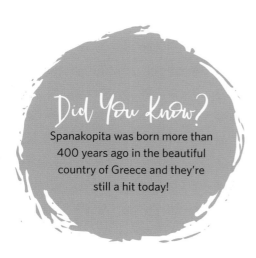

Did You Know?

Spanakopita was born more than 400 years ago in the beautiful country of Greece and they're still a hit today!

Green Bean Casserole (FASOLAKIA) SERVINGS: 4–5

Here you have Greek green beans in a gorgeous, lush tomato sauce. You're in for a treat. This recipe was and still is my favorite recipe. There is just something to be said about this combination, how warming it is and the memories that flow through my mind while making it!

2 tbsp (30 ml) extra virgin olive oil

1 medium yellow onion, diced

3 cloves garlic, roughly chopped

5 cups (500 g) green beans

3 medium-sized potatoes, cut into quarters then halved

½ cup (30 g) fresh parsley, roughly chopped

¼ cup (30 g) fresh mint, roughly chopped

1 zucchini, cut into 1-inch (2.5-cm) cubes

1 (13.5-oz [398-ml]) can roma tomatoes, unsalted

1 tsp coconut sugar

½ tsp tomato paste

Salt and pepper to taste

Boiling water to cover the mixture

In a deep pot heat the olive oil for a minute, then add the onion and garlic. Cook down on low heat until the onion is translucent. Add the beans and potatoes to the pot and cook them for about 3 minutes on medium heat, stirring occasionally to avoid burning. When the potatoes and beans begin to develop a nice golden color add the parsley, mint, zucchini, tomatoes, coconut sugar and tomato paste. Simmer this mixture for around 10 minutes, on medium heat, stirring often to avoid burning. Add salt and pepper to taste.

Increase the heat to high and add hot water to cover the beans and potatoes. Bring to a boil then simmer on low heat with a lid on for about 20 minutes. Make sure there is always water in the pot. You don't want this to be a soup-like dish but you definitely want some extra liquid so you can enjoy that beautiful sauce with a slice of bread at dinner!

This dish is traditionally enjoyed with feta so look for a plant-based feta to serve with this recipe!

Did You Know?

Green beans provide cellular energy, strengthen connective tissue, help build strong bones and protect against free-radical (pollution, smoking, etc.) damage. They are a great source of vitamin C, calcium and protein, which makes them a great healthy protector, antioxidant and an anti-inflammatory food!

Yummy Stuff (YEMISTA) SERVINGS: 4–5

YUMMMMMMMYSTUFFF!!!! This is what you call Yemista if you don't have a Greek background and have absolutely no clue what people are talking about when they ask you: "Would you like some yemista?" In that moment, right then, your life changed. I know stuffing vegetables is super popular right now but I assure you this Greek dish will leave you wanting more, in awe and genuinely just excited to eat more stuffed vegetables—from this book, duh.

1 large yellow onion, grated

4 large cloves garlic, grated

3 large tomatoes

2 large eggplants

4 large peppers, cut off tops and remove white veins on the inside

1 (14-oz [398-ml]) can roma tomatoes, unsalted

6 medium-sized russet potatoes: 2 peeled and cut into chunks, 4 cut into medium-sized wedges

⅓ cup (20 g) fresh mint, finely chopped

⅓ cup (20 g) fresh parsley, finely chopped

1 vegetable stock cube

1⅓ cups (250 g) jasmine rice

Salt and pepper to taste

8 tbsp (120 ml) extra virgin olive oil, divided

1 tbsp (3 g) oregano

Preheat the oven to 375°F (190°C) and set a large baking sheet aside.

Put the onion and garlic in a food processor. Pulse until the mixture looks as though you've grated it (you can grate instead if you prefer). Place the mixture in a large mixing bowl.

Cut off the tops of the tomatoes and gently remove the insides leaving around ½ inch (13 mm) from the outside of the tomato. Save the insides of the tomatoes and the tops. Find the side of the eggplant that sits flattest and cut a slice off the top of the opposite side. Gently remove the insides leaving around ½ inch (13 mm) from the outside of the eggplant. Set aside the insides and top of the eggplant. Cut off the tops of the peppers and remove the white veins and seeds on the inside. Set aside the tops of the peppers. Arrange the tomatoes, eggplant and peppers on a baking sheet.

Put the insides of the eggplant and the roma tomatoes in a food processor and process for about 30 seconds, or until there are no lumps. Transfer to the mixing bowl with the onion and garlic.

In the same food processor, add the potato chunks. Pulse until smooth. Transfer to the mixing bowl. Add the mint and parsley. Also add the stock cube and break it down as much as you can. Add the rice to the mixing bowl and stir well. Season with salt and pepper and sprinkle with 6 tablespoons (90 ml) of olive oil; stir well.

Spoon the stuffing mixture into the tomatoes, eggplant and pepper. Fill to the brim then cover with the top of each vegetable. Place the wedged potatoes around the stuffed vegetables and lightly season with more salt and pepper and the oregano.

If there is any liquid left in the bowl from the rice mixture, pour it into the base of the baking sheet along with the stuffed vegetables and potatoes—this is a game changer! Also add 1 cup (240 ml) of water to the pan. Drizzle the remaining 2 tablespoons (30 ml) of olive oil over everything. Bake in the oven for 1½ to 2 hours, until the rice is cooked and the potatoes are tender. Your house will smell amazing and your stomach will be growling!

Ass Patties (KOLOKITHOKEFTEDES) SERVINGS: 12–14

OOOF. What a mouthful. I'm sorry but do any of you know what you're about to make? If you don't, just try and think of it like this: You are about to eat GOLD. I wish you all were flies on the wall to witness my aunt and I mastering this recipe, vegan style, in the kitchen. It was like a Greek lady party and we were literally cheering with joy when we realized that the chickpea flour and cornstarch were the secret ingredients to perfecting these.

It's so easy to make, so super healthy and everyone will love it! This recipe pairs well with lemon, tzatziki and a side of love yourself because the food you eat does not have to control your mind.

3 large zucchini, grated

1 tsp sea salt

1 medium yellow onion, grated

2 cloves garlic, crushed

½ cup (30 g) fresh mint

⅓ cup (25 g) fresh cilantro

½ cup (46 g) chickpea flour

1 tbsp (8 g) cornstarch

½ tsp cumin

Pepper to taste

1–2 tbsp (15–30 ml) olive oil

Tzatziki (page 192)

Grate the zucchini into a medium-sized bowl. Add the salt and set aside for 5 minutes while you prepare your other ingredients.

Grate the onion into another large mixing bowl. Using your hands, squeeze out all the liquid. Make sure to get every last drop out. Discard the liquid. Add the garlic, mint, cilantro, chickpea flour, cornstarch, cumin and pepper. Stir gently and set aside.

After the zucchini has rested, using your hands, squeeze out all the liquid. Once you have managed to give your arms a work out and have removed all the liquid, add the zucchini to the large mixing bowl. Using your hands, mix well. Divide the mixture into about twelve equal portions and roll each into a ball. Then, flatten each ball into a little patty.

Warm the olive oil in a frying pan over high heat for about 1 minute—you want it to be smoking hot. Add six or seven little patties at a time and cook for about 4 minutes on each side. You will know when they are ready to flip when they are completely golden brown and not sticking to the bottom of the pan. Repeat until you've cooked all the patties.

Transfer the cooked patties to a plate covered with a paper towel and let them soak up the excess oil before serving hot or cold, with tzatziki.

Note

You may need to add more oil when you repeat the cooking steps; it depends on the frying pan you're using.

Protein-Packed Bean Soup (FASOLATHA)

SERVINGS: 4–5

This recipe is so easy! I promise all you need to do is a few things: 1. Soak your beans. 2. Boil your beans. 3. Add all this goodness to a pot and let it cook down for around an hour while you get on with your productive day. This dish is filled with protein, flavor and character. It goes so well with fluffy rice, steamed vegetables or naan bread. I loved eating this dish on a cold day when I was young. I was a figure skater growing up, so this type of meal was perfect to help warm me up and keep me fueled and energized for those 5 a.m. wake-up-calls. It also was a great source of protein, which is especially important after an intense training session!

1 cup (105 g) white navy beans, soaked overnight, drained

4 tbsp (60 ml) extra virgin olive oil

1 medium yellow onion, finely chopped

3 celery stalks, finely chopped

3 carrots, round chop

2 medium-sized potatoes, cubed

2 tsp (5 g) vegetable stock powder

1 cup (240 g) roma tomatoes, from a can, unsalted

2 bay leaves

6 cups (1.5 L) vegetable stock

1 red apple

Salt and pepper to taste

Place the beans in a large bowl, cover with water and soak for 12 to 24 hours. Drain the beans.

In a large pot bring the beans and about 6 cups (1.5 L) of water to a boil, then as soon as you see the first bubbles developing stop cooking. Drain your beans.

In a large pot over low heat, cook the olive oil, onion, celery, carrots, potatoes and vegetable stock powder for about 15 minutes. You do not want these to take any color, just simply to cook down to develop a good flavor base. Add the beans, roma tomatoes, bay leaves, vegetable stock, apple and salt and pepper to your pot. Bring to a boil then simmer on low heat with the lid on for 1 to 1½ hours. Check the soup occasionally during the cooking process and add more water if necessary. You don't want it to be too watery but you also do not want this to be like a stew! You will know the soup is done when the beans are tender and the vegetables are soft and breaking apart. The longer you let it cook, the more the flavor will develop.

Before serving, remove the apple and bay leaves. Enjoy with rice, bulgur wheat or Israeli couscous.

This soup is traditionally enjoyed with feta and olives.

In the Kitchen tip

Soaking your beans overnight not only decreases cooking time but increases digestibility by removing phytic acid, an anti-nutrient that makes legumes hard to digest and steals minerals from the body in the digestive process.

Warm Tomato & Spinach Rice Salad (SPANAKORIZO) SERVINGS: 4–5

Hello, we meet again, mouthful-name-of-a-recipe. This dish is pronounced SPA NA KO RIZO. I promise this recipe is amazing and I would have to say that this is probably the most popular recipe on my mom's side of the family. If my mom is short on ingredients and in a hurry then you better believe we are eating spanakorizo.

There are many different ways that I have seen this dish made. You have the option to leave out the tomato paste and instead add lemon; pick your flavor of choice—both options are fabulous and will leave you feeling more than 100% satisfied with yourself and your body!

3 tbsp (45 ml) extra virgin olive oil

1 medium yellow onion, finely chopped

1 green onion stem, finely chopped

½ cup (5 g) fresh dill

½ cup (30 g) fresh parsley

½ cup (120 ml) white wine

1 cup (185 g) white basmati rice

2 tbsp (33 g) tomato paste

5 cups (1.25 L) sodium-free vegetable stock or water

12 cups (360 g) fresh spinach (see note)

Salt and pepper to taste

In a saucepan, heat the olive oil over high heat for about 30 seconds until nice and hot. Turn the heat down to medium and add the onion and green onion. Let the onions sweat down for 3 to 4 minutes, or until translucent. Add the dill and parsley and give the mixture a good stir. Add the wine and cook until all of the wine has evaporated. Add the rice and tomato paste and stir well until fully combined. Turn the heat to high and add the vegetable stock. Bring to a boil then reduce the heat and simmer until the rice is nearly cooked, 20 to 25 minutes. Add the spinach and seasoning at the last minute. Wilt the spinach until reduced by half.

Serve hot and enjoy!

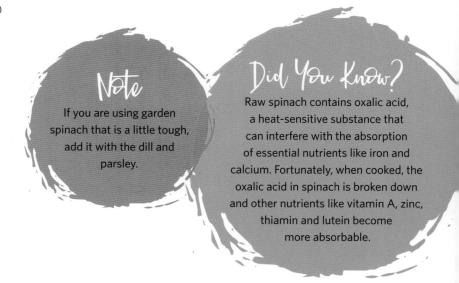

Note

If you are using garden spinach that is a little tough, add it with the dill and parsley.

Did You Know?

Raw spinach contains oxalic acid, a heat-sensitive substance that can interfere with the absorption of essential nutrients like iron and calcium. Fortunately, when cooked, the oxalic acid in spinach is broken down and other nutrients like vitamin A, zinc, thiamin and lutein become more absorbable.

Fuck Yes! Traditional Lentil Soup SERVINGS: 4–5

FUCK YES. Yep, that's what this recipe is called and I can tell you from experience that if you send your children to school with this dish and they ask their teacher for their "Fuck Yes" for lunch they will, indeed, end up in detention ... that is, until they get their mom to explain to the teacher that they're not making it up and that's what this soup is *actually called*! Can you tell my childhood was entertaining? *My Big Fat Greek Wedding* is no joke guys, you can't make this shit up.

This dish reminds me of my mom and her way with food. She can take any ingredients and turn them into a masterpiece. This recipe may seem so simple but I assure you that when those first bites hit your mouth your whole lentil world will change.

This dish is simple by nature so I don't like to fuss with any additions but if you want to go ahead and add some vegetables, or extra spices or seasonings then have at it but I keep this basic recipe close to my heart, just as it is.

2 cups (384 g) lentils

7 cups (1.7 L) water

¾ cup (180 g) roma tomatoes, from a can, unsalted (this is optional; don't add if using cumin)

1 vegetable stock cube

1 medium yellow onion, finely chopped

4 cloves garlic, whole

2 bay leaves

¼ tsp cumin powder (optional; don't add if using tomatoes)

Salt and pepper to taste

4 tbsp (60 ml) extra virgin olive oil

2 tbsp (30 ml) red wine vinegar

In a large bowl, soak the lentils in water for up to 24 hours but for at least 12. Drain and rinse the lentils, transfer to a large cooking pot and add water. Bring to a boil and simmer for about 20 minutes or until soft. Then drain and rinse again.

Put the lentils back in the pot and add 7 cups (1.7 L) of water, tomatoes (if not using cumin), stock cube, onion, garlic and bay leaves. Bring to a boil then lower the heat and simmer for about 1 hour with the lid on. Add the cumin (if not using tomato), salt and pepper. Cook for another 15 minutes with the lid on. Stir gently. Add the olive oil and vinegar. Cook for another 10 minutes with the lid on before serving.

Note

This soup tastes even more amazing the next day!

Did You Know?

Lentils are a great source of protein and fiber in a plant-based diet and could also be a key player in growing healthy locks. Lentils are packed with folate—containing 180 mcg per ½ cup (96 g)—a vitamin that restores the health of red blood cells, which provide hair follicles the oxygen they need to help your hair grow long and strong!

Traditional Greek Lemon Potatoes

SERVINGS: 4–5

These potatoes are on every Greek's most wanted list and if you've been to a Greek event you'll know that they're often the most raved about! Did I mention they're fabulous? This recipe is perfectly paired with a salad, gorgeous bean dish and a side of "who gives a shit if you're eating carbs, carbs have energy and you need energy to stay alive." One meal with potatoes will not push you off the wagon; if it took you years to get to where you are, one meal will not change a thing!

8 medium-sized potatoes, quartered

½ cup (120 ml) extra virgin olive oil

1 cup (240 ml) lemon juice

5 cloves garlic, pressed

1 tbsp (3 g) oregano

Salt and pepper to taste

Preheat the oven to 375°F (190°C) and line a baking sheet with parchment paper.

Put the potatoes, olive oil, lemon juice, garlic, oregano and salt and pepper in a large bowl and stir well. If you really want things to be out of bounds you could marinate this mixture for an hour before baking but if you're in a hurry just stir, transfer to the baking sheet and bake for about 35 minutes or until golden brown on the outside and steamy on the inside!

Serve hot with a fresh greens salad and tzatziki!

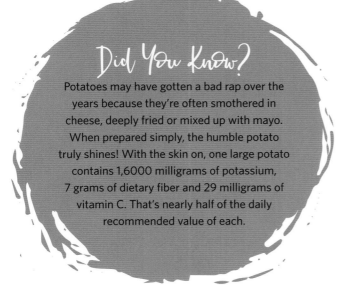

Did You Know?

Potatoes may have gotten a bad rap over the years because they're often smothered in cheese, deeply fried or mixed up with mayo. When prepared simply, the humble potato truly shines! With the skin on, one large potato contains 1,6000 milligrams of potassium, 7 grams of dietary fiber and 29 milligrams of vitamin C. That's nearly half of the daily recommended value of each.

Energy-Packed Salads

See, the thing is, eating salads does not have to be boring nor does it have to be just lettuce and oil. By combining a balanced amount of ingredients into salads you end up feeling fuller longer, happier about your food choices and probably more inclined to eat a salad again!

These salads are all very encouraging, some are easy to make but most importantly they'll teach you so much about the importance of a full-spectrum diet—sure to spike your eagerness to cook for yourself every day!

Years ago, when I was less sure of myself, self-conscious and afraid of food I would turn to salads for each and every meal. At one point, I was eating steamed bok choy for breakfast. I don't know what it was, the fact that I was no longer vomiting and I was proud and wanted to keep it up? Or the fact that I was getting skinny and I thought the only way to be/stay skinny was if I ate salad. I couldn't be more wrong. All the while I was a salad addict I was also miserable. So tired, not working and really not focused. Your body needs nourishment so by adding grains, bulgur or even seeds you are adding that little extra love that your body needs and truly deserves.

Salads are the safe zone but they're only good in the short run. Try some of these salads to develop a better understanding of how food can really change your mood and day!

Self-Love Buddha Bowl with Baked Falafel SERVINGS: 5

This salad is one of my favorites in this book for many reasons! It is basically four recipes all wrapped into one salad, not to mention it is nourishing and completely inspired by my Greek neighbors, the Turks. Turkish cuisine comes in second behind Greek (of course) and ahead of Lebanese. When it comes to cooking, I really stay close to the eastern Mediterranean—there is just something about this type of food that makes me feel so happy and satisfied.

This salad is flavorful, filled with texture and full of character. If you have picky eaters in the family I would highly recommend this recipe as you can pick and choose what you want to add to each bowl. Plus, this type of dish makes people happy! All the components are very simple, using amazing, beneficial ingredients that are nourishing for you and your family. Let the kids help by adding the ingredients into the processor or blender. This salad takes some time to make—but it is so worth the wait!

FALAFEL

1 (18-oz [540-ml]) can chickpeas, drained

1 small shallot, quartered

½ cup (55 g) carrot, grated

¼ cup (15 g) parsley

¼ cup (15 g) cilantro

1 tbsp (9 g) sesame seeds

1 tbsp (15 ml) extra virgin olive oil

Juice from ½ lemon

3 garlic cloves

1 tsp cumin powder

½ tsp pink Himalayan sea salt

¼ tsp fresh cracked black pepper

2 tbsp (12 g) chickpea flour

HUMMUS

1 (13.5-oz [400-ml]) can chickpeas, drained

4 tbsp (60 ml) olive oil

1 heaped tbsp (15 g) tahini

Juice of 1 lemon

Dash of red wine vinegar (thank me later!)

3 cloves garlic

½ tsp cumin

Salt and pepper to taste

¼–½ cup (43–86 g) cooked beetroot (optional, for beetroot hummus)

AVOCADO SALSA

2 ripe avocados, cut into cubes

¼ cup (40 g) yellow onion, grated

1 glove garlic, pressed

1 tbsp (15 ml) olive oil

2 tbsp (30 ml) lemon juice

¼ cup (15 g) fresh cilantro, finely chopped

Salt and pepper to taste

LEMON TAHINI DRIZZLE

6 tbsp (90 g) tahini

Juice of 1 large lemon

Zest from lemon

1 garlic clove, pressed

¼ cup (15 g) cilantro and parsley, finely chopped

½ cup (120 ml) water, plus more to thin out to desired consistency

Pinch of chili flakes

Salt and pepper to taste

CARBS + SALAD

2 cups (300 g) cooked barley, bulgur, quinoa or lentils

2 cups (32 g) red kale, cut into bite-sized pieces

2 cups (32 g) green kale, cut into bite-sized pieces

TOPPINGS

½ cup (70 g) black olives

¼ cup (35 g) roasted pine nuts

Fresh sprouts of choice

Handful of fresh mint

Handful of fresh parsley

Wedges of lemon

Sesame seeds

Cashew tzatziki (page 192)

To make the falafel, add the chickpeas, shallot, carrot, parsley, cilantro, sesame seeds, olive oil, lemon juice, garlic, cumin, sea salt and pepper to a food processor and blend until completely smooth (this may take a few minutes and make sure to smoosh down the sides of the processor). Transfer to a large mixing bowl. Add the chickpea flour and stir. If you find the mixture to still be quite light then add a bit more chickpea flour but only a ½ teaspoon at a time until you reach a thick enough consistency to bake or fry.

Let the mixture sit for at least 2 hours in the refrigerator covered with a small plate or plastic wrap.

Preheat the oven to 375°F (190°C). Line a baking sheet with parchment paper and grease with olive oil or cooking spray. Using an ice cream scoop, form little balls and roll them around until you get the perfect shape. Bake for 25 minutes or until a toothpick inserted comes out clean. Flip the balls halfway through the baking time.

To make the hummus, blend the chickpeas, olive oil, tahini, lemon juice, vinegar, garlic, cumin and salt and pepper in a strong food processor until creamy and smooth. If making beetroot hummus, add the beetroot with the other ingredients.

For the avocado salsa, mix the avocado, onion, garlic, olive oil, lemon juice, cilantro and salt and pepper in a small bowl until well-combined. Be gentle, avocados are sacred shit!

To make the lemon tahini drizzle, in a small bowl or container stir the tahini, lemon juice and zest, garlic, cilantro and parsley, water, chili flakes and salt and pepper until well-combined. If the mixture is too thick, add a teaspoon of water at a time. Store in an airtight container in the refrigerator for up to a week.

To assemble and serve your bowls, have all your salad ingredients ready in separate bowls, similar to an assembly food line or buffet. Start your bowl with your choice of carb or grain. Then add your kale, dressing and falafel. Top with your favorite toppings. Finish with a squeeze of lemon tahini drizzle and sesame seeds!

*See photo on page 76.

Did You Know?
Beetroot is a rich source of betaine, a natural liver detoxifier, digestive aid and bile thinner.

All Hail the Kale Caesar Salad
SERVINGS: 4

KALE YEAH, baby, we are about to make a bitchin' salad and it's the best, ever! Let's start by introducing the star of the show, the main character if you will . . . the lentil croutons. They are filled with flavor, add so much love to the dish and replace that extra crunch that traditional bread croutons would normally bring to the table. Now ya'll know I got nothing against carbs but sometimes it's okay to go for the substitute, after all it really helps you step outside the box and possibly explore other "crouton" options!

If you make this salad, add your desired amount of water to the dressing to meet your family's needs! I like my dressings a bit chunkier sometimes, so make it, check it and adjust! The leftover dressing will last up to 1 week in a tightly sealed container in the refrigerator.

COCONUT BACON

1 cup (93 g) flake unsweetened coconut

1 tbsp (15 ml) avocado oil

2 tbsp (30 ml) soy sauce

1 tbsp (15 ml) maple syrup

1 tsp smoked paprika

½ tsp liquid smoke

Salt and pepper to taste (more pepper than salt)

LENTIL CROUTONS

1 (15-oz [425-g]) can yellow lentils

1 tbsp (15 ml) extra virgin olive oil

3 tsp (10 ml) fresh lemon juice

1–2 tbsp (18–36 g) nutritional yeast

1 tbsp (3 g) dry dill

1 tsp parsley flakes

1 tsp garlic powder

1 tsp onion powder

Salt and pepper to taste

Cayenne to taste

CASHEW DRESSING

½ cup (70 g) cashews or cooked chickpeas

¼ cup (60 ml) extra virgin olive oil

¾–1 cup (180–240 ml) water (add more if you find the consistency isn't runny enough; keep it mind it will thicken up over time)

Juice of 1 large lemon

2 garlic cloves, pressed

2 tbsp (36 g) nutritional yeast

1 tbsp (9 g) capers

1 tsp onion powder

½ tsp Worcestershire (there are vegan brands on the market; I use Wizard)

Salt and pepper to taste

SALAD

1 large bunch of kale, washed, and chopped into bite-sized pieces

¼–½ cup (29–58 g) vegan mozzarella cheese (I use Daiya)

Thinly sliced kelp (optional but really adds that fishy taste traditional Caesars have!)

(continued)

ALL HAIL THE KALE CAESAR SALAD (CONTINUED)

Preheat the oven to 325°F (165°C). Line two large baking sheets with parchment paper.

In a bowl, combine the coconut flakes, avocado oil, soy sauce, maple syrup, paprika, liquid smoke and salt and pepper. Let them sit and marry while you are preparing the lentils.

Drain the lentils, gently patting them dry. Add them to a large bowl along with the olive oil, lemon juice, nutritional yeast, dill, parsley, garlic powder, onion powder, salt and pepper and cayenne. Stir until well-combined then transfer to a baking sheet. Make sure the lentils are evenly distributed across the baking sheet. This will help them get nice and crunchy! Cook for about 15 minutes. Remove from the oven, flip them with a spatula and return to the oven, rotating the baking sheet. Bake for another 15 minutes.

Transfer the coconut bacon to the second baking sheet. I use tongs to avoid bringing any extra liquid over to the baking sheet. Evenly distribute the coconut to ensure really crispy "bacon"! Cook for about 15 minutes, or until crispy, flipping halfway through.

While the lentils and coconut are cooking, add the cashews or chickpeas, olive oil, water, lemon juice, garlic, nutritional yeast, capers, onion powder, Worcestershire sauce and salt and pepper to a high-speed blender or food processor and blend until smooth. You can also use a handheld blender. Add more water as necessary if you like a thinner dressing.

Assemble your salad by adding the kale to a large mixing bowl. Mix in the dressing and stir till well combined, adding as much or as little dressing and you'd like. Transfer to a serving dish and top with the lentil croutons, coconut bacon, vegan mozzarella and kelp. This salad is going to blow your mind!

Did You Know?

Choosing oil with a high smoke point when cooking over high heat is important. When an oil starts to burn and smoke, beneficial nutrients are lost and harmful free radicals are created and released into your food. Avocado oil has the highest flash point of any cooking oil—a firey 520°F (270°C)!

Vietnamese Rice Noodle Salad

Oh, my lord, this salad is life. How many of you have gone out for Vietnamese, come home and thought to yourself "I wish I could make that at home BUT VEGAN?" Well, if you have, you're in luck! Here it is. Wakame (seaweed) is a great substitute for the fish sauce often used in Asian recipes. It's easy to make and even more fun to enjoy!

I really enjoy eating this dish for lunch as it is super fresh, fragrant and forgiving! Just make sure you add whatever you love and I promise it will turn out perfectly. The tofu is optional, so if you don't like it, skip it!

TOFU

1 tbsp (6 g) fresh lemongrass paste

1 clove garlic, pressed

Juice of 1 lime

2 tbsp (30 ml) soy sauce

1 tbsp (13 g) coconut sugar

1 (12-oz [340-g]) package firm tofu, cubed

2–3 tbsp (30–45 ml) coconut oil

DRESSING

½ cup (40 g) wakame

1 clove garlic, pressed

¼ cup (15 g) cilantro, finely chopped

1 jalapeño pepper, finely chopped

Juice of 1 lime

2 tbsp (26 g) coconut sugar

1 tbsp (15 ml) soy sauce

1 tbsp (6 g) fresh chili or 1 tsp dried (optional)

SALAD

1¾ cups (300 g) cooked rice vermicelli

2 cups (140 g) napa cabbage, thinly sliced

1 cup (128 g) carrot, julienned

¾ cup (78 g) cucumber, julienned

¼ cup (65 g) Thai basil, finely chopped

¼ cup (15 g) mint, fresh, finely chopped

¼ cup (18 g) green onions, finely chopped

Fresh lime

Chopped peanuts

Sriracha sauce

In a large mixing bowl, combine the lemongrass, garlic, lime juice, soy sauce and sugar. Cut the tofu into around 1-inch (2.5-cm) cubes. Add the tofu to the bowl and let marinate for 5 minutes.

In a large frying pan heat the coconut oil on high for around 30 seconds. Place the tofu in the pan using tongs (to avoid excess liquid) and cook for about 10 minutes, or until crispy on each side. Place the cooked tofu onto a cloth or paper towel to soak up any excess oil.

(continued)

VIETNAMESE RICE NOODLE SALAD (CONTINUED)

To make the "fish" sauce, boil the wakame and 2 cups (480 ml) of water in a small saucepan for 10 minutes. Strain out the seaweed, reserving the broth. Return the broth to the small saucepan and simmer until the broth has thickened. You want to have about 3 tablespoons (45 ml) of sauce.

Add the garlic, cilantro, jalapeño, lime juice, coconut sugar, soy sauce, chili (if using) and wakame liquid to a jar and blend using a whisk or simply by shaking. If you're using a whisk (which I recommend), just put the whisk in the jar and holding it straight up, grip tightly with both palms and simply roll your hands together as though you are trying to warm up. This is such a great trick and creates such a well-combined dressing!

Assemble your salad by adding the tofu, rice noodles, napa cabbage, carrots, cucumbers, Thai basil, mint and green onions to a bowl and giving it a gentle stir. I suggest individually dressing each serving of the salad—that way the salad doesn't go bad if you don't eat it all in one go.

Garnish with fresh lime, peanuts and Sriracha sauce!

Did You Know?

Wakame is an edible brown kelp that is common in Japanese, Korean and Chinese cuisines. This seaweed is a great source of bio-available magnesium, a mineral that most people lack. Studies show that adding more magnesium to one's diet provides natural relief for everything from severe menstrual cramps to bouts of depression to migraines and digestive disorders.

Summer Salad Rolls with Walnut Beef and Peanut Sauce SERVINGS: 4

A little twist on a classic salad roll is up next! I mean, come on, how excited are you to try out walnut beef? After adapting the recipe and practicing it a few times I finally came up with this goodie! These rolls are slightly time consuming but when they are made they are the *perfect* snack to bring along to school, work or on the road. They are super easy to stow away in a container and enjoy later when you're feeling up for a delicious snack. I highly recommend enjoying with the bad-ass peanut sauce I've suggested—it pairs perfectly with the slightly crunchy walnuts and fresh and creamy avocado and mango! Yum!

WALNUT BEEF

2 cups (200 g) crushed walnuts

Juice of 1 lime

3 tbsp (45 ml) soy sauce

1 tbsp (13 g) coconut sugar

½ tsp fresh grated fresh ginger

3 cloves garlic, pressed

1 tbsp (20 g) hot sauce

¼ tsp 5-spice powder

Salt and pepper to taste

SALAD ROLLS

10 rice paper rolls

3 cups (100 g) alfalfa sprouts or 3 cups (528 g) cooked white rice noodles

1 ripe mango, thinly sliced

1 large bunch of mint, thinly sliced

1 large bunch of cilantro, stems removed

1 large yellow pepper, cut into matchsticks

1 ripe avocado, thinly sliced

3 medium carrots, shredded

Spicy Chili Peanut Butter Lime Dressing (page 180)

In a medium-sized bowl, mix the walnuts, lime juice, soy sauce, coconut sugar, ginger, garlic, hot sauce, 5-spice powder and salt and pepper. Give the mixture a good stir and set aside.

Bring 4 cups (1 L) of water to a boil. Slice or cut any fillings you will be using. Arrange a preparation station with all your ingredients. Fill a large shallow dish with the boiling water and place a damp cloth next to it on the kitchen counter. Have a plate and another damp dish towel on hand.

When you are ready to assemble your rolls, dip the rice paper into the water just long enough to soften, 10 to 20 seconds, then quickly and gently transfer to the damp cloth. Add your desired fillings, then gently roll over once, fold in both sides and then roll again to seal the salad roll. Place onto a serving plate and cover with another damp, room temperature kitchen towel. Repeat above steps until you run out of toppings. Store leftovers covered in the refrigerator for 2 days.

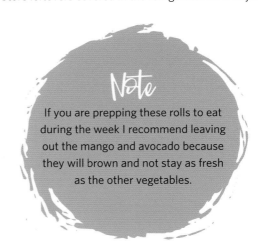

Note

If you are prepping these rolls to eat during the week I recommend leaving out the mango and avocado because they will brown and not stay as fresh as the other vegetables.

Bulgur Wheat Salad SERVINGS: 4

I love salad. I love eating healthy. I love loving my body and I love knowing I am making the right choices for my mind and my day. So I eat simple bulgar wheat salads to keep me fueled and energized. This salad is particularly easy because all you have to do is cook the bulgar, cut the veg, prepare the dressing and bam, you're done. Feel free to play around with the ingredients and have fun with it! And remember: By placing salads in jars you are not only helping the planet but you also feel fancy AF. Win-win!

1 cup (124 g) zucchini

Juice of 1 lemon

2–3 tbsp (30–45 ml) extra virgin olive oil

Salt and pepper to taste

3 cups (546 g) bulgur wheat, cooked according to package directions

1 cup (60 g) fresh parsley, finely chopped

½ cup (52 g) cucumber, cubed

½ cup (85 g) fresh tomatoes, roughly chopped

1 large stalk green onion, thinly sliced

1 clove garlic, pressed

2 tbsp (17 g) sunflower seeds

2 tbsp (8 g) pumpkin seeds

Using a mandoline or knife, cut the zucchini lengthwise into ½-inch (13-mm) strips. Season each side with a drizzle of olive oil and season with salt and pepper.

In a cast-iron grill pan or skillet, cook for about 4 minutes on each side, until nicely charred but still holding their shape. Cut into pieces and wait patiently to add to the salad!

In a small jar, put the lemon juice, olive oil and salt and pepper. Shake well.

In a large mixing bowl, toss together the bulgur wheat, parsley, cucumber, tomato, green onion, garlic, sunflower seeds and pumpkin seeds.

Pour an equal amount of dressing into four medium-sized mason jars. Scoop salad into each jar, leaving an inch (2.5 cm) at the top (room to shake).

Store in the refrigerator until ready to eat! Give it a good shake before eating.

Did You Know?

Bulgur is made from wheat berries that have been parboiled, dried and cracked into tiny bits. A Mediterranean staple, this nutritious grain has a delicious, nutty flavor and cooks quickly. One full cup (182 g) provides 8 grams of fiber; 6 grams of protein; and minerals like manganese, magnesium and iron.

Creamy Orzo Pasta Salad

This recipe is filled with healthy fats, carbs and greens but the best part is that you don't have to feel restricted with it. Use anything you have in your fridge and spice it up to your liking. You can also eat it warm or cold. I personally love it warm because the pasta and veggies get nice and creamy and the lemon is extremely aromatic, plus it makes it very comforting in the winter months!

3 cups (360 g) cooked orzo

1 cup (150 g) cherry tomatoes

1 cup (140 g) roasted red pepper

1 cup (30 g) spinach, finely chopped

½ cup (75 g) yellow pepper, cut thinly lengthwise

½ cup (70 g) raw almonds, toasted on a cast-iron skillet for 10 minutes on medium heat, roughly chop once cooled

¼ cup (3 g) fresh dill

¼ cup (35 g) black olives

1 tbsp (8 g) capers

Creamy Greek "Feta" and Oregano Dressing (page 183)

In a large mixing bowl, toss together the orzo, cherry tomatoes, red pepper, spinach, yellow pepper, almonds, dill, black olives and capers.

Pour an equal amount of dressing into four medium-sized mason jars. Scoop salad into each jar, leaving an inch (2.5 cm) at the top (room to shake).

Store in the refrigerator until ready to eat! Give it a good shake before eating!

Did You Know?

Greek orzo, called "kritharaki," is made from a different type of durum wheat and can vary in size. Kritharaki means "little barley" in Greek, as reference to this tiny pasta being the shape of an unprocessed grain of barley.

Israeli Couscous Salad

SERVINGS: 3–4

Welcome to your next go-to salad recipe; it's perfect on-the-go, as a dinner side or great as a light snack! You'll fall in love with the simplicity of this salad but you'll come back for the tangy lemon flavor and hints of the Mediterranean.

3 cups (470 g) cooked Israeli couscous

3 tbsp (45 ml) olive oil

1 (15-oz [420-g]) can organic chickpeas, drained and rinsed

Juice and zest of 1 large lemon

¼ cup (15 g) fresh cilantro, very finely chopped

½ cup (5 g) fresh dill, very finely chopped

½ cup (30 g) fresh parsley, very finely chopped

½ cup (87 g) pomegranate seeds

1 cup (55 g) microgreens, your favorite will do!

Salt and pepper to taste

In a large bowl, add the couscous, olive oil, chickpeas, lemon juice and zest, cilantro, dill, parsley, pomegranate seeds, microgreens and salt and pepper and stir until well-combined and coated. Garnish with more fresh herbs, an additional squeeze of lemon and drizzling of your finest olive oil!

Scoop the salad into four medium-sized mason jars, leaving an inch (2.5 cm) at the top (room to shake).

Store in the refrigerator until ready to eat!

Did You Know?

Not only are pomegranate seeds high in vitamin C and vitamin K, they could do wonders for gut health. Research suggests that several bioactive compounds contained in pomegranates stimulate probiotic bacteria production, thus strengthening digestion and enhancing the body's ability to fight bacterial infection.

the Works! Fully Loaded Quinoa Greek Salad

SERVINGS: 4

I am back at it again with the Greek salad stuff but this time I present to you the salad I ate so often I almost made myself hate it. It's so addicting, so easy and really foolproof. It combines the latest trends with the roots of my childhood—and that can't be a bad thing!

Let's just touch on a few things before you move on to the least boring salad ever. I used to think salads were lettuce, lettuce and more lettuce with a light dressing and a sprinkling of hate your body, so eat this shit, Maria. It took me a while to figure out that I was so wrong and that salads can have so many different varieties of greens + veggies. They can even have carbs. You can even have DRESSING that doesn't taste like air mixed with gluten-free water, can you believe it? Simple ingredients like olive oil do have the calories we've all been "taught" to be afraid of but I promise you things like olive oil, quinoa, capers and artichokes are what your body is calling out for. Hair growth, nail strength, soft skin and more benefits are to be expected when you just enjoy the right foods, eat balanced and legit just love the fuck out of yourself!

½ cup (80 g) red onion, thinly sliced

3 tbsp (45 ml) extra virgin olive oil

Juice of 1 large lemon

Salt and pepper to taste

2 cups (370 g) cooked quinoa

1 (13.5-oz [400-ml]) can white beans, drained

1 cup (150 g) cherry tomatoes, halved

1 cup (104 g) mini cucumber, chopped

½ cup (70 g) olives, halved

¼ cup (14 g) sundried tomatoes, halved

¼ cup (34 g) capers

¼ cup (42 g) artichoke hearts, quartered

Creamy Greek "Feta" and Oregano Dressing (page 183)

Soak the red onions in enough lemon juice or apple cider vinegar to cover for 10 minutes. Drain. (You can reserve the soaking liquid for the next time you make this recipe, use in another recipe or just discard.)

Whisk the olive oil, lemon juice and salt and pepper in a small bowl (or shake in a small jar).

On a large serving dish, decoratively arrange the quinoa, white beans, cherry tomatoes, cucumber, olives, sundried tomatoes, capers and artichoke hearts. (Refer to the picture for ideas on how to arrange the ingredients.) Drizzle with the prepared dressing. For a more casual dinner, simply add all your ingredients to a mixing bowl and give it a good stir.

If you plan on having some of this salad throughout the week then keep the veggies and white beans separate from the quinoa and dressing—this will help it last longer!

Easy Thai-Infused Coleslaw Salad SERVINGS: 4

This salad is balanced, filled with flavor, easy to make and perfect for lunch, dinner or even a snack. It's also a bit of Thailand in the comfort of your own home. Five years ago, I went to Thailand, got way too drunk and ate all the good food. I was so inspired but at that point I was still afraid. That trip changed my life, forever. I met the love of my life, probably came home with more than one parasite and learned the building blocks of self-love.

I dedicate this salad to anyone out there who is still fighting. Your fight is never over, unless you let it be. You deserve to live. You deserve to love. You deserve to be loved. I promise you it gets better, you just have to find it within yourself to love the person you are. Accept yourself. Forgive yourself. Be kind to yourself. Change won't happen overnight but over time you will get better.

Here is something that helped me through the struggles of recovering from bulimia: Nothing is permanent but change. If you don't like what you see in the mirror one day just remind yourself that it can change. You can move forward, make the right choices and slowly become yourself again. Reminding myself that in that moment it doesn't matter was the best thing that's ever happened to me.

4 cups (64 g) black kale, finely sliced

2 cups (180 g) green cabbage, finely sliced

2 large carrots, grated

1 cup (63 g) sugar snap peas, cut widthwise on a diagonal

2 stems green onion, finely chopped

½ cup (30 g) fresh cilantro

¼ cup (36 g) roasted peanuts

2 tbsp (18 g) sunflower seeds

Diced chilies, add as much as you like (optional)

Spicy Chili Peanut Butter Lime Dressing (page 180), thin out to desired consistency

Add the kale, cabbage, carrots, snap peas, onion, cilantro, peanuts, sunflower seeds, chilies and dressing to a large mixing bowl and stir gently.

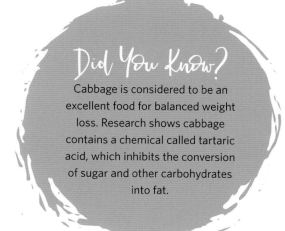

Did You Know?

Cabbage is considered to be an excellent food for balanced weight loss. Research shows cabbage contains a chemical called tartaric acid, which inhibits the conversion of sugar and other carbohydrates into fat.

Cool Cabbage and Seed Salad   SERVINGS: 4

Last summer, Andrew and I went to Nicaragua where we enjoyed beautiful weather, amazing people and ever better food. So many amazing dishes entered our bellies but one thing really stuck with me: cabbage. I fell in love with soaked cabbage while I was there.

I know it's known for causing gas but if you just soak the cut cabbage in water and a bit of salt for a few hours before making the salad then it should help. I'm not joking, I ate cabbage every day and was strutting around in my bikini 24/7—no shame, no bloat and no problems. I highly suggest you try this recipe—you can even sub out the seeds and modify them according to your cycle, this is called "seed cycling" and it's amazing. Seed cycling can help balance your hormones and get your menstrual cycle back on track! (It helped me after coming off birth control!) Here's how it works: For the first 2 weeks of your cycle eat 1 tablespoon (10 g) each of pumpkin and flaxseeds every day. For the last 2 weeks of your cycle eat 1 tablespoon (10 g) each of sesame and sunflower seeds every day.

½ medium-sized head green cabbage, cut extremely thin and soaked (see above)

Juice of 2 large limes

2 tbsp (30 ml) olive oil

1 cup (60 g) fresh cilantro, very finely sliced

½ cup (5 g) dill, very finely sliced, or 2 tbsp (6 g) dill weed

Salt and pepper to taste (I like this one on the salty side)

¼ cup (35 g) sunflower seeds

¼ cup (16 g) pumpkin seeds

In a large mixing bowl, combine the cabbage, lime juice, olive oil, cilantro, dill, salt and pepper, sunflower seeds and pumpkin seeds and stir until well-combined. Let the salad rest for 5 to 10 minutes before serving.

Did You Know?

The Egyptians would eat cabbage with vinegar before a night of drinking to prevent a groggy morning after! Cabbage contains minerals that help the liver metabolize alcohol more easily and it is still today considered one of the best remedies to cure a hangover.

Falling in Love with Breakfast

Breakfast time is the most important meal of the day and my favorite time to be alone and think. It's when I retaught myself how to think, see and understand food. Throughout my early life, I never ate breakfast. I never woke up hungry! I didn't really care if I ate in the morning because I didn't understand the importance of breakfast.

I had no idea that eating breakfast would help change my digestive system, mood and even my attention span. As the days went on I would literally jump out of bed hungry. It was such a strange thing for me but I eventually developed such an intense desire for breakfast that it actually ended up making me happy. I was going to the bathroom better, being more productive and my body was actually noticeably changing too! I was losing weight around my belly, holding onto muscle better and my immunity was rock solid!

I realize we all know that breakfast is the "most important meal of the day" but do we actually take that saying literally? I hope you do because if you don't, you're really missing out!

Green Waffles with Creamy Corn Salsa SERVINGS: 4–6

This breakfast is for all my savory lovers. When I was recovering from bulimia it was really hard to even think about eating a heavy breakfast, let alone waffles. This recipe is really important to me because I realized eating waffles does not have to be bad for you. Instead you can take zucchini and spelt flour and make a beautiful meal to start your day!

WAFFLES

2 tbsp (15 g) ground flaxseed, 6 tbsp (90 ml) warm water

1 cup (384 g) zucchini, grated and put through cheesecloth or cloth to remove all water

½ cup (80 g) yellow onion, grated

2 cloves garlic, pressed

¼ cup (15 g) cilantro, very finely chopped

1 tbsp (15 ml) extra virgin olive oil

Salt and pepper to taste

1 cup (120 g) spelt flour

1 cup (160 g) oats

1 tbsp (15 g) baking powder

½–¾ cup (120–180 ml) almond milk, unsweetened

WARM CORN SAUCE

1 tbsp (15 ml) extra virgin olive oil

½ cup (80 g) yellow onion, finely chopped

2 garlic cloves, finely chopped

2 cups (330 g) yellow corn, steamed or roasted

Salt and pepper to taste

1 small jalapeño, diced and seeded

¼ cup (15 g) cilantro, finely chopped

Few leaves of basil, cut finely, lengthwise

1 (13.5-oz [400-ml]) can full-fat coconut milk

Add the ground flaxseed and water to a small ramekin. Give it a little stir and let it sit for about 10 minutes.

Add the zucchini, onion, garlic, cilantro, olive oil, salt and pepper, spelt flour, oats, baking powder and almond milk to a large mixing bowl and stir until well-combined. (Start with ¼ cup [60 ml] almond milk and add up to ½ cup [120 ml] to reach a really moist-on-the-inside waffle, adding 1 tablespoon [15ml] at a time.) Fold in the flaxseed mixture then stir one last time, making sure there are no lumps.

Heat your waffle maker; when hot, spray with coconut oil. Use a ladle to spoon the waffle batter onto the waffle maker and cook for about 5 minutes or until golden brown. Repeat this process, including spraying with coconut oil, with the rest of the batter. Keep the waffles warm on a plate or baking sheet in the oven set on very low heat while the rest of them cook and you prepare the corn sauce.

While the waffles are cooking, make the corn sauce. In a medium-sized pan or skillet, heat the olive oil for 30 seconds. Add the onion and cook down on medium heat until translucent. Add your garlic and corn and cook over medium to low heat for about 10 minutes, or until the corn is soft and tender. Add the salt and pepper, jalapeño, cilantro and basil and cook for another 10 minutes on low. Add the coconut milk and cook for another few minutes or until hot throughout.

Dollop the warm corn sauce onto your waffles and thank me later!

Did You Know?

It is believed that spelt flour was first used about 8,000 years ago, making it one of the oldest cultivated crops in human history! With a nutty and slightly sweet flavor, spelt is a grain related closely to wheat but containing less gluten and more protein.

the Perfect Pumpkin Pancakes

When Andrew and I lived in London I would make him pancakes almost every weekend. At first, it was really hard for me to enjoy them without freaking out and panicking about sugars and carbs. After months I perfected a similar recipe to this one and learned that you don't always need sugar to make foods taste fabulous. Instead you can use nature's candy to add nutrients, character and flavor!

1 tsp chia seeds

½ cup (123 ml) + 1 tbsp (15 ml) canned pumpkin purée, unsweetened and organic

⅓ cup (75 g) banana, mashed, overripe

1 tsp vanilla

¾ cup (180 ml) coconut milk, from a carton, unsweetened

¼ cup (60 ml) maple syrup

2 tbsp (30 ml) coconut oil, melted (plus more for cooking)

1½ cups (188 g) all-purpose flour

¼ cup (30 g) spelt flour

¼ cup (30 g) almond flour

1 tsp cinnamon

2 tsp (9 g) baking soda

¼ tsp nutmeg

¼ tsp salt

⅓ cup (55 g) vegan chocolate chips

Vanilla dairy-free yogurt

Walnuts

Maple syrup

In a small bowl or ramekin, combine the chia seeds with 3 tablespoons (45 ml) of warm water. Allow the mixture to set for 3 to 5 minutes, or until a jelly-like consistency develops.

In a small mixing bowl, stir the pumpkin, banana, vanilla, coconut milk, maple syrup and coconut oil until well-combined. Add the chia mixture and stir well.

In a large mixing bowl, combine the flour, spelt flour, almond flour, cinnamon, baking soda, nutmeg, salt and chocolate chips. Stir well, watching for flour lumps, and then create a small well in the middle of the bowl. Transfer the wet ingredients into the bowl with the dry ingredients and stir well.

Using small amounts of coconut oil, about 1 teaspoon, heat a nonstick pan over medium to low heat. When the oil is hot, form small pancakes using a small ice cream scoop. Cook for about 2 minutes on each side. Top with yogurt, walnuts and maple syrup.

Did You Know?

If you want to boost the health of your hair, skin and nails then consider incorporating flaxseed into your diet. The alpha-linolenic acid (ALA) benefits skin and hair by providing essential fats as well as B vitamins, which can help reduce dryness and flakiness. So if you want to add a few tablespoons of flaxseed to this recipe, have at it!

Carrot Banana Crumble Muffins SERVINGS: 10

Muffins were always a frightening "food group" for me. I mean, how could something that looks so beautiful and delicious possibly be good for you? Of course, some muffins are indeed nourishing and great for you and your body, but more times than others you will find that muffins have loads of processed ingredients, extra sugar and unnecessary fillers. Over the years I have become more and more comfortable with muffins, cupcakes and delicious treats, but I must say, nothing beats homemade!

For the record, I believe in balance, so if you want that muffin in the window, then baby girl you better fucking eat it!

1 tsp chia seeds

2 cup (240 g) spelt flour

½ cup (60 g) almond flour

2 tsp (9 g) baking powder

1 tsp baking powder

½ tsp baking soda

1 tsp cinnamon

¼ tsp ginger powder

¼ tsp salt

½ cup (113 g) ripe banana, mashed (about 1 medium banana)

1 cup (110 g) grated carrots

2 tbsp (30 ml) coconut oil, melted

4 tbsp (60 ml) maple syrup

1–1½ cups (240–360 ml) non-dairy milk, unsweetened

1 tbsp (15 ml) vanilla extract (good quality)

½ cup (50 g) crushed walnuts or dairy-free chocolate chips

1 tsp apple cider vinegar

CRUMBLE TOPPING

4 tbsp (52 g) coconut sugar

½ cup (42 g) rolled oats

4 tsp (18 g) coconut oil, melted

1 tsp cinnamon

Preheat the oven to 375°F (190°C) and spray a regular-size muffin tin with coconut oil. I would suggest using a silicon muffin tray for easy removal!

In a small bowl or ramekin, combine the chia seeds with 3 tablespoons (45 ml) of warm water. Allow the mixture to set for 3 to 5 minutes, or until a jelly-like consistency develops.

Sift the spelt flour, almond flour, baking powder, baking soda, cinnamon, ginger and salt into a large bowl and stir well.

In a medium-sized bowl, stir the banana, carrots, coconut oil, maple syrup, milk (start with 1 cup [240 ml] and add more as needed), vanilla, walnuts or chocolate chips and vinegar until well-combined. Add the chia mixture and fold through gently.

Transfer the wet ingredients into the dry ingredients and fold through until well combined; there should be no flour around the sides.

Using a small ice cream scoop fill each muffin cup to the top. Set aside.

Add the coconut sugar, rolled oats, coconut oil and cinnamon to a small bowl and stir. Using a teaspoon, sprinkle the topping over each muffin. Be as generous as you'd like, just save some for each guy!

Bake for 18 to 22 minutes, then enjoy!

Did You Know?

Coconut sugar is derived from the coconut palm and is known for its nutrient density and low glycemic index. Notable nutrients found in coconut sugar include iron, zinc, calcium and potassium. Who said sugar had to be empty calories?!

Breakfast Cake SERVINGS: 8

Cake, cake, cake . . . you know what I like? Cake! I was addicted to cake when I was young. I particularly had an intense addiction to ice cream cake from Dairy Queen but that was short lived because of my eating disorder. I went through a phase where I wouldn't eat or even think about something from a fast-food shop or even foods that came in a box. I have a tendency to take things to the extreme so I wasn't surprised by this phase in my life, but I am glad I came out of it. I started playing with ingredients likes dates, nuts, seeds, fruits and plant-based milks to come up with the perfect cake I could eat throughout the day without feeling like a sack of shit. And want to know what? By learning how to use these ingredients I also learned to love the body I live in and the food I eat.

3 cups (525 g) pitted Medjool dates

1 cup (84 g) rolled oats

½ cup (72 g) raw almonds

½ cup (58 g) raw hazelnuts

1 tbsp (15 ml) maple syrup

2 tbsp (10 g) cacao powder

½ cup (120 ml) unsweetened coconut milk from carton

2 tsp (10 ml) vanilla

1½ cups (210 g) raw cashews

1½ cups (365 g) frozen bananas

1 cup (255 g) frozen strawberries

Fresh berries

Edible flowers

Line the base of a 9-inch (23-cm) springform pan with parchment. Soak the dates in warm water for 5 minutes.

In a food processor, blend the dates, oats, almonds, hazelnuts, maple syrup and cacao powder until a large ball forms, or until well-combined. You should still be able to see the nuts but make sure the dates are nice and smooth! Place the filling in the springform pan and using your hands flatten out the base. You can use a cup or mug to make sure everything is even. Place in the freezer while you make the rest of the cake.

Put the coconut milk, vanilla, cashews, bananas and strawberries in a high-speed blender and blend until smooth, about 2 minutes. You may have to swoosh down the sides of the blender a few times to make sure everything is well-blended. Remove the base from the freezer, and pour the filling into the pan. To flatten the filling, slam the pan down on a counter or table a couple times. If you have no stress to release just use the back of a spoon.

Freeze for at least 3 hours, or preferably overnight.

Decorate with fresh berries and edible flowers to make it beautiful. You can refer to my photo for inspiration! Enjoy!

The cake will keep in the freezer, covered with plastic wrap, for up to a week!

Stuffed Avocado with Fresh Pico de Gallo

SERVINGS: 4

While I lived in London I was diagnosed with irritable bowel syndrome (IBS). It sucked trying to stay positive while not feeling like I was restricting my diet. The IBS FODMAP, a list of foods to avoid, was horrible to read or even look at and it felt like I was spiraling down into another eating disorder. I knew I did not want that to happen so I did research every day and figured, screw the map, your body can handle this, you just need to figure out how to train it. This recipe is one of the first recipes I made to eat for breakfast at work and at home on the weekends.

Garlic and onion suck for IBS but I figured my mental health was far more important to me, so I sucked it up and dealt with the constipation and bloating that go along with eating these ingredients. I eventually became strong enough to deal with dietary food restrictions associated with my IBS and gut health.

The dish is very tropical and Latin-inspired. It's simple with lots of heat, lemon and spice. I love enjoying this dish with brunch or on crackers!

2 large, ripe, avocados

1 tsp extra virgin olive oil (optional)

PICO DE GALLO

1 tbsp (15 ml) olive oil

3 tomatoes, seeded, small dice (I used roma)

½ sweet white onion, small dice

1 green pepper, seeded, small dice

½ jalapeño, seeded, small dice (if you like it spicy add some of the seeds)

1 clove garlic, minced or pressed

¼ cup (15 g) cilantro, finely chopped

Juice of 2 limes

Salt and pepper to taste

Halve the avocados, remove the pits and remove some avocado from the middle to make room for your pico! (TIP: Add the extra avocado to a creamy smoothie, it'll make it super delish!)

In a large bowl, mix the olive oil, tomatoes, onion, green pepper, jalapeño, garlic, cilantro, lime juice and salt and pepper. Stir lightly and taste test for seasoning.

Stuff the avocados with pico and drizzle with olive oil if you'd like. You can enjoy these alongside loads of different breakfasts. Things like smoothies and burritos would be awesome!

Did You Know?

Avocados are truly a superfood, with studies showing benefits from decreasing inflammation to insulin regulation and weight loss. The majority of fat in an avocado is monounsaturated—a type of fat that is actually heart healthy!

Ultra—Simple Banana Bread SERVINGS: 8-10

Oh, banana bread we meet again. You basically got me through living in England and for more than one reason. I would make you every night. I would distract myself, hidden again in the kitchen making you, while my whole heart knew I was unhappy and either needed to go home or make some big changes.

This recipe is the first recipe I perfected—I genuinely love this banana bread sooo much. It makes me so happy, helps me feel good and brings back so many memories of living across the pond, where FoodByMaria was born.

This banana bread is on the gooey side but that's how I like it! Feel free to add just a tad less banana (1 cup [150 g]) to achieve a more traditional consistency.

2 cups (240 g) spelt flour

¾ cup (150 g) coconut sugar

1¼ tsp baking powder

1 tsp baking soda

1 tsp cinnamon powder

½ cup (84 g) dark chocolate chips

½ tsp salt

1 flax egg (1 tbsp [15 g] ground flaxseeds and 3 tbsp [45 ml] hot water)

1 cup (240 ml) almond milk, unsweetened

1½ cups (225 mg) banana, mashed, ripe (almost brown)

1 tsp vanilla extract

Preheat the oven to 375°F (190°C). Grease a 9 x 5-inch (23 x 13-cm) bread tin with coconut spray.

In a large mixing, bowl stir the spelt flour, coconut sugar, baking powder, baking soda, cinnamon, chocolate chips and salt.

Put the ground flaxseeds and hot water in a small bowl or jar. Let sit for about 5 minutes or until gooey and egg-like.

In a small mixing bowl, stir the almond milk, banana and vanilla just until combined (don't overstir). Add the wet ingredients to the dry ingredients bowl. Stir until there are no more flour clumps but make sure not to overstir. I like using a spatula to fold, this helps prevent overstirring!

Transfer the batter to the prepared tin and bake for 45 to 55 minutes, or until a toothpick inserted into the center comes out clean.

Enjoy hot with vegan butter or cold anytime!

Caramelized Bananas & Chocolate Chip Oats

SERVINGS: 2–3

YUMMY!! This breakfast was hands down my ultra-addiction throughout the whole time I was in London. I would literally go to bed dreaming about oats and a lot of the time I would jump out of bed in the morning (yep, the girl who used to cry at the thought of food *is now excited to eat*!) just because I could not wait to eat this simple, delicious breakfast!

It took a while to figure out but after a bit of trial and error I realized that my body needed a more heavy/dense breakfast in the mornings to get my digestive system going. I love adding flaxseeds to my breakfast as a natural aid to keeping me light, energized and ready to take on the day!

1 cup (84 g) oats

2–3 cups (480–720 ml) hot water or nondairy milk

1 tbsp (7 g) flaxseeds

3 tbsp (45 ml) coconut oil, melted, divided

1 tbsp (11 g) nondairy chocolate chips or toasted cacao nibs

Dash of maple syrup

2 bananas, halved lengthwise

1 tbsp (13 g) coconut sugar

Slivered almonds

Nut butter

Blueberries

In a small or medium pot, bring the oats, water or milk, flaxseeds, 1 tablespoon (15 ml) of coconut oil, chocolate chips and maple syrup to a boil, then lower the heat and cook on low until the oats are completely cooked. This may take 5 to 10 minutes, depending on your oats of choice. I like using quick oats because I wake up super hungry and want to eat right away!

While the oats are cooking, heat 2 tablespoons (30 ml) of coconut oil in a medium-sized frying pan for 30 seconds. Place the halved bananas in the frying pan, cut-side down, and cook for about 1 minute on each side. Be patient when flipping to ensure the perfect form. If not cooked enough the banana will stick and if cooked too much it will melt into deliciousness (although that is not a bad thing!).

Add your oats to a bowl, then add your gorgeous banana and toppings! Enjoy!

Did You Know?

Like all grains, oats have anti-nutrients that block mineral absorption in the gut and can cause bloating or indigestion for those with sensitive stomachs. To get the most out of this powerhouse brekkie, soak your oats overnight in a bowl of water + 1 teaspoon of apple cider vinegar or lemon juice then rinse in a colander in the morning. This extra step will keep your belly happy and make the oats more digestible and nutritious!

Confident Kick Black Bean & Sweet Potato Breakfast Burrito SERVINGS: 4

This breakfast is perfect for hangovers. Now let me be clear. I am not telling you to go out and get drunk, but I am 100% saying that if you responsibly indulge in alcohol here and there, that this breakfast would *certainly* aid in your morning after recovery and add lots of love to that empty alcohol-broken soul of yours.

I no longer drink that much and when I do (every quarter, ha) I die for 3 days. So, don't worry, you can still enjoy this on any ol' regular day or family gathering!

I love these burritos because they are sweet from the sweet potatoes, creamy from the avocados and have a hint of freshness from the cilantro and tomato.

3 tbsp (45 ml) extra virgin olive oil, divided

1 small yellow onion, half finely diced, half sliced, divided

2 cloves garlic, pressed

1 (20-oz [591-ml]) can black beans, drained

Juice of 1 lime

Dash of salt and pepper

½–1 tsp cumin

½ tsp coriander

1 cup (240 ml) vegetable stock, no sodium

1 large sweet potato, peeled and cut into 1-inch (2.5-cm) cubes

½ tsp garlic powder

½ tsp turmeric

½ tsp cinnamon

1 tsp maple syrup

Dash of cayenne pepper

4 tortillas, brown or ancient grain

1 cup (195 g) cooked white rice

½ cup (55 g) vegan cheese of choice

1 ripe avocado, chopped or mashed

1 cup (180 g) fresh tomato, seeds removed, cubed

1 cup (60 g) lightly packed fresh cilantro

In a small pot or cast-iron skillet, heat 1 tablespoon (15 ml) of olive oil over medium heat. Add half of the onion, the pressed garlic, black beans, lime juice, salt and pepper, cumin, coriander and vegetable stock. Cook for 25 to 30 minutes on medium heat. Let the mixture cool, then blend in a food processor until smooth.

In another large cast-iron skillet or frying pan heat 2 tablespoons (30 ml) of olive oil over medium heat. Add the sliced onion, sweet potato, garlic powder, turmeric, cinnamon, maple syrup and cayenne pepper. Cook on medium heat for about 20 minutes, stirring occasionally to avoid burning. You can cover with a lid that's slightly smaller than the pan you're using to further the cooking process. This also helps with caramelization!

Assemble by spreading the black beans on the tortilla, then add the rice, cheese, sweet potatoes, avocados, tomato and cilantro. Finish off by grilling the rolled burrito in a panini press for a few minutes (this is optional; if you don't have a press you could just use a pan). Enjoy!

Rise & Shine Smoothie Bowl with Homemade Granola

Fitness, staying active and always moving was a huge part of my life while recovering from bulimia. I admit at times I probably took things too far (typical Pisces me) and overdid it a bit, but now I have found balance and I know when to relax and listen to my body's needs. I love this smoothie before or after my early-morning workout. It's filled with texture, loaded with nutrients but most importantly it's easy to make. Simple recipes were very important to me throughout recovery because I knew that I needed to eat well but I didn't always have the time. This recipe is a two-in-one, for sure!

GRANOLA

2 cups (168 g) old-fashioned rolled oats (use gluten-free if you'd like)

¾ cup (75 g) nuts (I use almonds, pecan and walnuts)

½ tsp sea salt

¼ cup (60 ml) coconut oil, melted

¼ cup (60 ml) maple syrup

¼ cup (74 g) coconut flakes, unsweetened

¼ cup (25 g) dairy-free chocolate chips (optional)

SMOOTHIE BOWL

1 cup (240 ml) plant-based milk

½ cup (128 g) frozen mango

½ cup (128 g) frozen strawberries

1 frozen banana

1 tsp acai

Dash of vanilla extract

TOPPING OPTIONS

Coconut yogurt, unsweetened

Fresh strawberries

Fresh mango

Chunky peanut butter

Fresh nuts and seeds

Drizzling of maple syrup

Preheat the oven to 350°F (175°C) and line a baking sheet with parchment.

Add the oats, nuts, sea salt, coconut oil, maple syrup and coconut flakes to a large mixing bowl. Stir them well and pour onto the baking sheet. Bake for 20 to 25 minutes or until golden brown. Let the granola cool then mix in the chocolate chips, if using.

For the smoothie, place the milk, mango, strawberries, banana, acai and vanilla in a high-speed blender and blend until smooth, about 1 minute.

Pour the smoothie into a bowl, adding the cooled granola and any topping you'd like!

Store the remaining granola in an airtight container at room temperature for up to 2 weeks.

Did You Know?

Acai powder is the richest known natural source of antioxidants (possibly beating out dark berries like blueberries, cranberries and strawberries)! This beauty is native to the Amazon and packed with beautiful benefits like essential vitamins, minerals and fiber! Feel free to add acai to all smoothies and juices—you won't regret it!

Creamy Autumn Chia Pudding

SERVINGS: 4

Super simple is what I am about. Combining the power of beautiful chia seeds, amazing toppings and healthy fats like coconut milk, it's the most balanced, nourishing and powerhouse breakfast ever. Did I mention it takes 10 minutes (plus soaking time) to make? Good. I have your attention now! The toppings are the center of attention and the best part is you can play around with what you know your family likes. There are no rules in the kitchen, just make sure you are having fun, eating responsibly and being kind to yourself and your body when it comes to your choices!

3–4 tbsp (30–40 g) chia seeds (if you like it thick add 4, if you like it thin add 3)

1 (13.5-oz [400-ml]) can of light coconut milk

1 tbsp (15 ml) maple syrup or coconut nectar

Dash of vanilla

1 tbsp (15 g) vegan butter

1 apple, cut into cubes

2 tbsp (8 g) pumpkin seeds

1 tbsp (13 g) coconut sugar

Dash of lemon juice

Dash of vanilla

½ tsp cinnamon

In a mason jar or tightly sealed container, add the chia seeds, coconut milk, maple syrup and vanilla. Let the mixture rest in the refrigerator for about 1 hour.

In a cast-iron skillet, warm the vegan butter over medium heat. Add the apple, pumpkin seeds, coconut sugar, lemon juice, vanilla and cinnamon. Cook over medium heat until golden and fragrant, around 10 minutes. Stir occasionally to ensure the mixture does not burn.

Top the chia pudding with the apple mixture and enjoy!

Did You Know?

Chia seeds were a staple food in the diets of the Aztecs and Mayans. Derived from the Mayan word for "strength," chia contains all eight essential amino acids and a whopping 4.7 grams of complete plant protein per ounce!

Rich & Fruity Chia Pudding SERVINGS: 4

This is a taste of the tropics in the comfort of your own home. I know this combination is becoming increasingly more popular but I first fell in love with it while visiting Nicaragua. Imagine you're sitting in a lounger, looking out upon the ocean and enjoying a gorgeous breakfast. Hear the waves crashing and admire the peaceful silence in the air.

3–4 tbsp (30–40 g) chia seeds (if you like it thick add 4, if you like it thin add 3)

1 (13.5-oz [400-ml]) can of light coconut milk

1 tbsp (15 ml) maple syrup

1 tsp cinnamon

Dash of vanilla

TOPPINGS
½ cup (90 g) mango, sliced

½ cup (91 g) apple, cut into matchsticks

1 passion fruit

Sprinkling of coconut flakes

In a mason jar or tightly sealed container, add the chia seeds, coconut milk, maple syrup, cinnamon and vanilla. Let the mixture rest in the refrigerator for about 1 hour.

Top your chia pudding with toppings and enjoy!

Did You Know?

Chia is super high in fiber, providing nearly 11 grams per ounce! The rich fiber content of this tiny seed helps you feel fuller quicker and supports healthy weight loss. Bonus: The "gel"-like substance that surrounds the seed when it contacts liquid works in the body as a prebiotic, supporting the growth of probiotics in the gut.

My Weekender Hash Browns SERVINGS: 4

Hash browns remind me of my dad. When I was young I would help in the kitchen at the restaurant (mostly just watching him and the cooks do their thing) and I remember always being fascinated by the browning of the potatoes. I mean who doesn't love a crispy potato?

This recipe holds a close place in my heart, but like all things in life we must change and adapt. I went with the less traditional hash by using sweet potato. This substitution helps with cooking time and even more so the way your body metabolizes the healthy, natural sugars in the sweet potato versus the good ol' regular white potato. It's important to know that every food can be adapted into a healthier version of itself. This was a very important lesson for me while overcoming bulimia and still wanting to enjoy good food while trying to overcome my fear of what food would do to me and my body.

2 tbsp (30 ml) extra virgin olive oil

1 medium onion, roughly chopped

3 cloves garlic, finely chopped

3 large sweet potatoes, peeled, cut into 1-inch (2.5-cm) cubes (can use white potato but may take longer to cook)

Dash of paprika

Salt and pepper to taste

½ cup (75 g) red pepper, small dice

½ cup (75 g) yellow pepper, small dice

¼ cup (18 g) green onion, finely chopped (plus extra for garnish)

1 cup (110 g) vegan cheddar cheese

4 tbsp (60 g) vegan sour cream

Warm the olive oil in a cast-iron skillet or large frying pan over medium heat. Add the onion and garlic. Cook down on low heat for about 1 minute, then add the potatoes, paprika, salt and pepper. Give this mixture a good stir then cover with a lid, leaving a bit of room for steam to escape. Cook for about 10 minutes. Add the red and yellow peppers and green onion. Cook for another 10 minutes. The potatoes should be golden and crunchy and the onions should be completely caramelized and soft.

Check the potatoes with a fork to make sure they are cooked through. Serve with cheese, sour cream and green onions! YUM!

Did You Know?

Vitamins A, D, E and K are fat-soluble, meaning your body only absorbs them in the presence of a fat. Combining nutrient-dense vegetables (like sweet potatoes) with a high-quality fat source such as olive oil, coconut oil or tahini will allow the body to reap the most nutritional benefits.

Ultimate Gooey Energy Bites

SERVINGS: 12–14

Andrew calls these "The Maria Gold Line Energy Balls." He compares them to the luxurious Ferrero Rocher chocolate hazelnut treats but without the added sugar and bullshit. He is a pretty particular man so to have him fall this deeply in love means something! They're totally worth a go.

For me, these energy bites symbolize a lot of things. They are the food I would turn to when I was confused, crying and unsure whether I should eat my next meal. They were always a safe snack (in some cases a real replacement) when I was weak but knew I needed to eat and keep that shit down.

1½ cups (263 g) Medjool dates, pitted

¾ cup (105 g) raw cashews or almonds

⅓ cup (44 g) macadamia nuts

⅓ cup (33 g) walnuts or pecans

1 tbsp (15 ml) coconut oil, melted

1 tbsp (5 g) cacao powder

1 tbsp (10 g) chia seeds

1 tbsp (7 g) flaxseeds

¾ cup (100 g) dark chocolate, melted (optional)

Soaked the dates for 5 minutes in warm water.

Pulse the cashews or almonds, macadamia nuts and walnuts or pecans in a food processor for a few seconds. Add the soaked dates, coconut oil, cacao powder, chia seeds and flaxseeds and blend for about 20 seconds. You may need to scrape down the sides of the processor to make sure everything is well-blended. You know you're done when your mixture forms a ball or becomes more difficult to blend.

Using a tablespoon or measurement tool of your choice begin form your little energy balls! Sometimes getting your hands a little bit wet will help you shape the balls.

If you would like to really spice these up, dip them into melted chocolate! Make sure the balls are cold when dipping into the melted chocolate! Then, place them on a plate lined with parchment paper and pop them into the refrigerator or freezer until firm.

Store in an airtight container for up to 3 weeks in the refrigerator or 3 months in the freezer.

Did You Know?

Macadamia nuts are rich in oleic acid, which plays an important role in reducing inflammation and boosting memory power.

Super Power Chaga Latte

HELLO, ADRENAL GODDESS, YOU! Chaga, you are life and I am so thankful for you but especially during the summer of 2017. This drink kept me sane, helped me power through my stressful workload but most importantly, made me relearn the art of self-love and self-awareness. Sometimes in life you think because you've overcome some big obstacles—like bulimia—that you become indestructible. Well, I couldn't have been more wrong. I crashed pretty badly the spring/summer of 2017 and turned to chaga and other mushrooms to help heal myself from the horrible symptoms I was going through, all because I didn't listen to the obvious, loud, first signs of adrenal fatigue.

This drink is perfect for everyone but especially for my hard-working go-getters.

1 cup (240 ml) cashew, almond or coconut milk (refer to homemade recipes on pages 151, 147 and 148)

1 tsp chaga or reishi

½ tsp maca powder

¼ tsp cinnamon

⅛ tsp turmeric powder

1 tsp maple syrup (optional if you're using one of my homemade milks)

1 tsp coconut oil, melted

In a small saucepan mix the milk, chaga or reishi, maca powder, cinnamon, turmeric, maple syrup and coconut oil. Heat over medium heat for about 5 minutes, or until the milk begins to bubble.

Transfer mixture to a high-speed blender and blend for 1 minute (to create some bad-ass froth).

Pour into mug and enjoy hot! Feel the calm, baby.

Did You Know?

Chaga mushrooms are one of the richest sources of beta-glucans, which can dramatically help strengthen and reinforce the body's immune response. Chaga is also anti-inflammatory, which makes it an ideal supplement for those suffering from IBS, colitis, arthritis, tendonitis and acne.

Must-Make Anti-Inflammatory Golden Milk

Did I mention I had IBS symptoms, suffered with ovarian cysts, had issues with bloating and suffered with severe constipation and bellyaches? Well, it bloody sucked! When I was teaching my body how to eat food again/keep it down, a lot of issues surfaced. Like learning to digest my food. That was hard for me as I was bloated 24/7—I'm not kidding—and when you're bloated do you want to eat? Nope. This is a recipe for danger and disaster, right? Once I was strong enough to set aside my mentality and start focusing on the physical side of things (the huge swollen bubble living in my abdomen/stomach) I began doing more research about things I could eat and drink to help ease the pain and symptoms.

This recipe was my savior; it worked so well I even got Andrew hooked on it! Not only is it good for you, it tastes glorious and is really easy to whip up! You can even make extra and heat it in the mornings!

Try drinking this healing milk before bedtime to allow your body to reap the anti-inflammatory benefits overnight!

3 cups (720 ml) plain, light coconut milk

1½ tsp (5 g) grated turmeric or good quality turmeric powder

¼–½ tsp ground ginger

¼–½ tsp cinnamon

1½ tbsp (23 ml) coconut oil, melted

1 tbsp (15 ml) maple syrup (optional if you're using my homemade coconut milk)

Pinch ground black pepper

In a small pan over low heat, stir the coconut milk, turmeric, ginger, cinnamon, coconut oil, maple syrup and black pepper. Cook on low heat for 3 to 5 minutes, using a whisk or spoon to combine. Make sure you do not bring the mixture to a boil.

Split this gorgeous mixture into two glasses and enjoy immediately! You can store it in the refrigerator if you like to prepare for morning drinks ahead of time, but know they will only last for up to 2 days.

Did You Know?

Turmeric is a powerful healing root that has been used for its antioxidant and anti-inflammatory properties for thousands of years. Studies have shown that black pepper increases the body's absorption of turmeric when the two are consumed together.

Kickin' It Snickers Bar Smoothie   SERVINGS: 2

We all know Snickers bars taste like summer holidays with George Clooney, so imagine what it must taste like in smoothie form—that's right, DELICIOUS! Sometimes I think smoothies get a bad rap for being filled with too many greens or too many fruits, but in this case this smoothie tastes like everything they tell you not to eat but still maintains the nourishing and good-for-you status.

Filled with protein, natural sweetness and antioxidants, this smoothie is guaranteed to kick that craving and stimulate those taste buds! This smoothie has worked wonders when it comes to keeping my daily diet balanced, when I may have overdone it on the salads and grains. Let's remember, I suffered from an eating disorder for 6 years. That shit doesn't just disappear, so as quickly as I fought it I can accidentally start things back up again. Drinking cheeky smoothies that I know are good for me helps keep my mind in check, knowing I am not restricting my body or my mind.

2–3 cups (480–720 ml) light coconut milk (add more or less depending on if you like runny or thick)

1 frozen banana

5 ice cubes

4 large Medjool dates, pitted

½ cup (70 g) raw cashews

1 heaped tbsp (17 g) peanut butter

1 tsp coconut oil, melted (see In the Kitchen Tip)

1 tsp coconut nectar or maple syrup

Dash of vanilla or ½ tsp vanilla powder

Peanut chunks (optional)

Dark chocolate shavings

Fresh berries

In a high-speed blender, mix the coconut milk, banana, ice cubes, dates, cashews, peanut butter, coconut oil, coconut nectar or maple syrup and vanilla on high until completely smooth. Top with peanuts, chocolate and fresh berries!

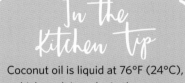

In the Kitchen Tip

Coconut oil is liquid at 76°F (24°C), which explains why in the warmer months your oil is soft and colder months hard as a rock. To avoid an oil clump in your smoothie, slowly add the oil while the blender is running and behold the creamy goodness!

the Two Best Friends Smoothie SERVINGS: 2

For as long as I can remember I have loved the chocolate and peanut butter combo, but if I'm being honest I didn't really know what a smoothie was until I was around 24 and I don't think I started to like them until I was 27. This smoothie is so luscious, perfectly sweet and great for those early mornings when you just don't have the time to put a proper breakfast together—although I would definitely recommend this bad boy paired with a chia pudding. It's little fundamental recipe building blocks like this one that have helped keep my mind and soul really grounded and constantly focusing on my well-being versus what the mirror is telling me. After all, breakfast and snacks are the most important "meals" of the day!

3 cups (720 ml) light coconut milk or almond milk

2 large frozen bananas, cut into 3-inch (8-cm) chunks

1½ heaped tbsp (8 g) cacao powder

2 tbsp (20 g) chia seeds

2 heaped tbsp (34 g) peanut butter

1 tbsp (15 ml) coconut nectar (optional)

1 tsp vanilla

OPTIONAL ADD-INS

1 tsp chaga

1 tsp reishi

1 tsp maca

1 tsp baobab

1 tsp ashwagandha

In a high-speed blender mix the milk, bananas, cacao powder, chia seeds, peanut butter, coconut nectar, vanilla and optional additions of your choice on high until smooth. Enjoy!

In the Kitchen Tip

Turn the jar upside down for a bit before opening to stir.

Did You Know?

Avoid added sugars, oils and preservatives in your nut butters by checking the ingredients list before you dig your spoon into the jar. The only ingredients listed should be peanuts/nuts and salt.

Fueling & Refreshing Beverages

These juices will sort out that weeklong hangover, reenergize that temple of a body of yours and keep you fueled and ready to do it all over again this weekend (if that's your thing).

I know juicing has been a trend for a while, but I also understand that not all of us have time to juice, clean the juicer and then store it all away until the next time. We've all been there—we think about juicing, but realize all the effort we'd have to put in and then our laziness kicks into overdrive. So as a solution, I came up with juices that are juicer-free.

Here's your cue to jump in joy, and thank me because now, you can spend more time in the sun, and less time inside cleaning up your juicing concoction. You're welcome.

The following drinks helped me stay creative in the kitchen while resting assured I was receiving all the liquids, nutrients and vitamins my body needed to get through my fun-filled, busy day!

Fresh Mint, Berry, Watermelon & Lime Juice SERVINGS: 4

Hey baby, I am the electrolyte digestion dream and I have come here to satisfy your thirst and refresh your senses! This juice is perfect for the spring and summer seasons. It is great for the family and kids or even for ladies' night (I won't judge you if you add adult water—we all thought about it).

35 oz (1 L) water

2 cups (408 g) ripe watermelon, cubed

1 cup (255 g) strawberries (can be frozen)

Juice from 3 limes

½ cup (30 g) fresh mint

Dash of maple syrup

1-inch (2.5-cm) cube fresh ginger

1 tsp pitaya powder (optional)

Pinch of sea salt (optional)

Add the water, watermelon, strawberries, lime juice, mint, maple syrup, ginger, pitaya powder and salt to a high-speed blender and blend for about 2 minutes or until completely smooth. Let the juice set in the refrigerator for 20 minutes before enjoying (unless you used very cold water).

Store in a jug or bottle, in the refrigerator, for up to 5 days!

Notes

If you like your juices more pungent and strong, then add a bit less water but if you're like me and want a bit more juice with a balanced flavor, be sure to add the full amount of water! Also, the juice may take on a brownish color. This is just from the mint, don't panic—it still tastes awesome!

Did You Know?

When we sweat, we lose electrolytes that cannot be replaced by water alone. If left unchecked, an electrolyte imbalance can lead to headaches, dizziness, muscle cramping and nausea—hello dehydration! This tasty watermelon elixir provides the electrolytes and support your body is craving without any added sugar or weird dyes.

Turmeric Celery Chia Water

YOU. NEED. TO. DRINK. THIS. JUICE. Drink it in the morning, on an empty stomach and reap the benefits. This juice will help heal your gut, strengthen your bones and purify your blood. This is perfect if you're looking for a natural detox and some anti-inflammatory aid (see below for more info) if you suffer from an eating condition or intolerance!

35 oz (1 L) water

Juice of 2 lemons

¾ cup (75 g) celery, chopped

1 cup (60 g) fresh mint

2 cups (354 g) honeydew or cantaloupe, cubed (could also be frozen)

1 tsp turmeric powder

Dash of maple syrup

½ tsp cayenne (optional; add more to taste)

1 tbsp (10 g) chia seeds

Add the water, lemon juice, celery, mint, honeydew, turmeric, maple syrup and cayenne to a high-speed blender and blend for about 2 minutes or until completely smooth.

Pour the mixture through a nut milk bag or a piece of cheesecloth into a large bowl to catch all that goodness. Use one hand to grip tight at the top of the nut milk bag (or gathered-up cheesecloth) while the other pushes the mixture through (this is super relaxing for me). Once you've strained all the liquid, transfer to a large bottle and add the chia seeds. Give it a good shake, then let the juice set in the refrigerator for 20 minutes before enjoying (unless you used very cold water). You can use the leftover pulp in smoothies!

Store in a bottle, in the refrigerator, for up to a week!

*See photo on page 136.

Note

If you like your juices more pungent and strong, then add a bit less water but if you're like me and want a bit more juice with a balanced flavor, be sure to add the full amount of water!

Did You Know?

The discomforts of acid reflux, bloating and indigestion are often caused by low stomach acid—celery juice to the rescue! The juice of this alkalizing veggie has been known to naturally raise stomach acid levels, allowing your body to properly digest and absorb the minerals and vitamins in your food. Drink this tonic on an empty stomach first thing in the morning to prime yourself for digestive bliss the rest of the day.

The Greek Green Goddess

SERVINGS: 4

This green juice is a punch of health and that added zing from the jalapeño is really a game changer. I know not all of us have the time to create a beautiful green salad all the time, so when you're in a time crunch but want that extra bit of nourishment, this recipe will be your go-to! Make extra because this shit is good.

35 oz (1 L) water

Juice of 1 lemon

Juice of 1 lime

¼ cup (15 g) fresh mint

¼ cup (15 g) fresh parsley

2 cups (218 g) apple, cut into quarters

2 cups (32 g) kale, chopped

1 cup (104 g) cucumber, cubed

1 tbsp (15 ml) maple syrup

1-inch (2.5-cm) cube fresh ginger

1-inch (2.5-cm) jalapeño, seeds removed (this is optional and if you do use it, add as much as you and your family can handle)

1 tsp spirulina (optional)

Add the water, lemon juice, lime juice, mint, parsley, apple, kale, cucumber, maple syrup, ginger, jalapeño and spirulina to a high-speed blender and blend for about 2 minutes or until completely smooth.

Pour the mixture through a nut milk bag or a piece of cheesecloth into a large bowl to catch all that goodness. Use one hand to grip tight at the top of the nut milk bag (or gathered-up cheesecloth) while the other pushes the mixture through (this is super relaxing for me). Once you've strained all the liquid, let the juice set in the refrigerator for 20 minutes before enjoying (unless you used very cold water). You can use the leftover pulp in smoothies!

Store in a bottle, in the refrigerator, for up to a week!

*See photo on page 136.

Note

If you like your juices more pungent and strong, then add a bit less water but if you're like me and want a bit more juice with a balanced flavor, be sure to add the full amount of water!

Did You Know?

Parsley is a member of the Umbelliferae family, along with carrots, dill, celery, fennel, coriander and cumin. This leafy green herb isn't just for garnishing! It has long been used to naturally treat urinary tract infections and kidney stones. Parsley contains two powerful healing compounds, myristicin and apiole, that act as a natural diuretic in removing infection-causing bacteria from the urinary tract.

Gingery Orange Explosion SERVINGS: 4

The beauty, skin and digestion juice is lovely to look at and easy to drink! It may seem super cliché but enjoying this juice a few times a week will work wonders for your energy, complexion and bowel movements.

Not only is this a super simple recipe, but it's also wicked healthy for you too. With all of us so focused on the daily grind, I reckon this juicer-less juice will serve us well, as we'll no longer have to sacrifice convenience for nutrition.

Step back juicer, you met your maker—and he comes with a nut milk bag.

35 oz (1 L) water

2 cups (256 g) carrots, cubed

2 cups (360 g) orange, peeled

1 apple, cubed

½ cup (30 g) fresh mint

1-inch (2.5-cm) cube fresh ginger

½-inch (13-mm) cube fresh turmeric

Dash of maple syrup

Add the water, carrots, orange, apple, mint, ginger, turmeric and maple syrup to a high-speed blender and blend for about 2 minutes or until completely smooth.

Pour the mixture through a nut milk bag or a piece of cheesecloth into a large bowl to catch all that goodness. Use one hand to grip tight at the top of the nut milk bag (or gathered-up cheesecloth) while the other pushes the mixture through (this is super relaxing for me). Once you've strained all the liquid, let the juice set in the refrigerator for 20 minutes before enjoying (unless you used very cold water). You can use the leftover pulp in smoothies!

Store in a bottle, in the refrigerator, for up to a week!

Note

If you like your juices more pungent and strong, then add a bit less water but if you're like me and want a bit more juice with a balanced flavor, be sure to add the full amount of water!

Did You Know?

Carrots are high in potassium and beta-carotene, which help improve skin tone, reducing dryness, blemishes and redness. Turmeric is not only a powerful anti-inflammatory but has been revered for its ability to correct oily skin; reduce signs of aging; speed up healing; and calm symptoms of eczema, psoriasis and other skin conditions.

Apple Pie Juice SERVINGS: 4

So, basically, if you put apple pie into a blender . . . you'd be drinking this flavorful dream! It's sweet, it's tangy and it's creamy. This juice is the best way to trick your fussy eaters into drinking something *extremely* nourishing. Read the Did You Know? to find out why you must make this juice and eat your walnuts, tomatoes and celery!

35 oz (1 L) water

2 cups (300 g) raw sweet potato, cut into 1-inch (2.5-cm) cubes

2 cups (308 g) ripe peaches, sliced

1 cup (110 g) green apple, sliced

1 tbsp (2 g) cinnamon

1 tsp nutmeg

Dash of maple syrup

Add the water, sweet potatoes, peaches, apple, cinnamon, nutmeg and maple syrup to a high-speed blender and blend for about 2 minutes or until completely smooth.

Pour the mixture through a nut milk bag or a piece of cheesecloth into a large bowl to catch all that goodness. Use one hand to grip tight at the top of the nut milk bag (or gathered-up cheesecloth) while the other pushes the mixture through (this is super relaxing for me). Once you've strained all the liquid, let the juice set in the refrigerator for 20 minutes before enjoying (unless you used very cold water). You can use the leftover pulp in smoothies!

Store in a bottle, in the refrigerator, for up to a week!

Note

If you like your juices more pungent and strong, then add a bit less water but if you're like me and want a bit more juice with a balanced flavor, be sure to add the full amount of water!

Did You Know?

When a food resembles a bodily organ that it nourishes or heals it's called the Doctrine of Signatures. The oblong sweet potato bears a strong resemblance to the pancreas, and also happens to be one of the best foods for promoting healthy function of this organ. Sweet potato juice is a powerful blood-sugar balancer and supporter of healthy hormone function. Other examples of this phenomenon include walnuts and the brain, tomatoes and the heart and celery and bones.

Almond Milk SERVINGS: 5

Who would have thought making your own fresh milk could be so easy? It's as simple as soaking, draining and blending! That's it. I love adding this fresh almond milk to my lattes, chagas, matchas and more. It's light, filled with protein and flavor.

1 cup (157 g) raw almonds, soaked in water for at least 8 hours

35 oz (1 L) water

3-4 dates or 1-2 tbsp (15-30 ml) maple syrup (optional)

Dash of cinnamon (personally I like adding more)

Blend the almonds, water, dates or maple syrup (if using) and cinnamon in a high-speed blender until completely smooth (this can take up to 90 seconds). Check the consistency of the liquid. It should be silky smooth, with no large chunks.

Run the milk through a cheesecloth or nut milk bag. Save the pulp for smoothies or cookies.

Pour the milk into a jug or bottle and store in refrigerator up to 3 to 5 days (but good luck, it never lasts that long for me!).

Note

To make strawberry or chocolate milk simply add about 6 strawberries or 2 tablespoons (10 g) of cacao powder!

Did You Know?

Soaking the raw nuts ahead of time activates beneficial enzymes, and thus may enhance your body's ability to digest and absorb nutrients such as vitamins A and C. Soaking also saturates the nut from the inside out, resulting in a creamier textured milk. You will also end up with more liquid because fully saturated nuts blend better, leaving behind less pulp!

Coconut Milk SERVINGS: 5

I love my coconut milk with oatmeal in the morning. I also add this coconut milk to pastas, carby meals and more. I typically don't use coconut milk in anything but cooking and leave the lighter milks for my coffees, teas and matchas.

1½ cups (140 g) unsweetened desiccated coconut flakes

35 oz (1 L) hot water

3–4 dates or 1–2 tbsp (15–30 ml) maple syrup (optional)

Dash of cinnamon (personally I like adding more)

Place the coconut in a heatproof bowl and add the hot water. Stir the mixture and allow it to cool to room temperature.

Blend the coconut mixture, dates or maple syrup (if using) and cinnamon in a high-speed blender and blend until completely smooth (this can take up to 90 seconds).

Check the consistency of the liquid. It should be silky smooth, with no large chunks.

Run the milk through a cheesecloth or nut milk bag. Save the pulp for smoothies or cookies.

Pour the milk into a jug or bottle and store in the refrigerator up to 3 to 5 days (but good luck, it never lasts that long for me!). Enjoy!

Note

To make strawberry or chocolate milk simply add about 6 strawberries or 2 tablespoons (10 g) of cacao powder!

Did You Know?

Coconuts are one of the best sources of lauric acid—a medium-chain triglyceride (MCT) that possesses antiviral and antibacterial attributes that help the body fight disease. The MCTs found in coconut milk are used by the body to increase energy expenditure and help enhance physical performance, making it a great pre- or postworkout choice!

Cashew Milk SERVINGS: 5

This is the perfect creamer substitute, especially if you are the kind of person who loves a luscious hot drink in the morning. Make sure you are extra aggressive with your nut milk bag with this recipe though, those cashews have a serious texture and you don't want any of that graininess in your coffee in the morning!

1 cup (140 g) raw cashews, soaked for 3 hours

35 oz (1 L) water

3-4 dates or 1-2 tbsp (15–30 ml) maple syrup (optional)

Dash of cinnamon (personally I like adding more)

Blend the cashews, water, dates or maple syrup (if using) and cinnamon in a high-speed blender and blend until completely smooth (this can take up to 90 seconds).

Check the consistency of the liquid. It should be silky smooth, with no large chunks.

For cashew milk, straining is optional! Cashew milk is the creamiest of all the homemade milks and depending on your blender and soaking time, you will rarely have to strain, thereby reaping all the fiber and nutritional benefits of the nut. This makes cashew milk less hassle and less waste! If you do want to strain, you can run the milk through a cheesecloth or nut milk bag. Save the pulp for smoothies or cookies.

Pour the milk into a jug or bottle and store in the refrigerator up to 3 to 5 days (but good luck, it never lasts that long for me!). Enjoy!

Note

To make strawberry or chocolate milk simply add about 6 strawberries or 2 tablespoons (10 g) of cacao powder!

Did You Know?

Grown widely in tropical regions around the world, cashews come from the cashew apple tree. The cashew apple has a delicate skin and a short shelf life, therefore is rarely exported fresh. The sharp-tasting, delicate apple from which each cashew nut grows is considered a healing delicacy and traditionally consumed for its natural medicinal qualities.

Oat Milk SERVINGS: 5

This is a less traditional milk but still delicious. I highly suggest this for your children, or for yourself when on your period or if you're feeling unwell. It's filled with fiber, nutrients and it's a great way to stay fuller longer.

1¼ cups (104 g) oats (I used quick oats)

35 oz (1 L) water

3–4 dates or 1–2 tbsp (15–30 ml) maple syrup (optional)

Dash of cinnamon (personally I like adding more)

Blend the oats, water, dates or maple syrup (if using) and cinnamon in a high-speed blender and blend until completely smooth (this can take up to 90 seconds).

Check the consistency of the liquid. It should be silky smooth, with no large chunks.

Run the milk through a cheesecloth or nut milk bag. Save the pulp for smoothies or cookies.

Pour the milk into a jug or bottle and store in the refrigerator up to 3 to 5 days (but good luck, it never lasts that long for me!). Enjoy!

Note

To make strawberry or chocolate milk simply add about 6 strawberries or 2 tablespoons (10 g) of cacao powder!

Did You Know?

This plant-based milk is an excellent option for anyone with a nut allergy or who is looking for a more budget-friendly alternative. Oat milk is an excellent source of calcium, potassium, vitamin E and folic acid. Oats also have skin-clearing properties and drinking oat milk has been known to clear acne and improve the overall health of the skin.

Treat Yourself, You Deserve It

For as long as I can remember, dessert has been the enemy in my overflowing mind. The dreaded moment when the waitress would tip-toe her return after taking our dinner plates was often my cue to get up and walk away and not until she had left the table was if safe to return. I didn't like the temptation. I am still not entirely sure where the fear first developed but I actually find it quite funny now because I don't like dessert that much. I am the savory gal!

All the recipes in this chapter really stimulate my senses and give that young-woman fear in me a smack in the face because they are obnoxiously simple, nourishing and bomb as fuck. Most of them do not require sugar and when they do it's coconut or organic brown. I always emphasize balance in my diet, so if you want that carrot cake, baby girl, then make it the right damn way!

These desserts are here to remind you that you only live once and that substitutes do exist. You don't have to feel shitty after your sugar crash, so instead, try one of these recipes and feel fabulous!

Strawberry Ice Cream Cake SERVINGS: 6–8

This cake is the perfect "sweet" treat to wow all your guests! It is made using no added sugar and all-natural, nourishing ingredients that are sure to stimulate your taste buds and leave you wanting more. This is best for a summer party, friendly gathering or just as a snack to have stowed away for those "I am craving..." moments.

2 cups (350 g) pitted Medjool dates

¾ cup (105) raw almonds

¾ cup (75 g) raw walnuts

1 tbsp (15 ml) organic brown rice syrup

1 tsp vanilla

1 cup (145 g) strawberries, washed, tops removed and halved

2 cups (280 g) raw cashews

¼ cup (60 ml) plant-based milk of choice

¼ cup (60 ml) maple syrup or coconut nectar

Dash of vanilla

Pitaya powder (optional, but adds an amazing pink color)

1 cup fresh berries of choice

Line an 8 x 8-inch (20 x 20-cm) cake tin with parchment (leave extra parchment hanging over on two sides, which will help you pat down the mixture).

In a food processor blend the dates, almonds, walnuts, brown rice syrup and vanilla for about 30 seconds or until only a few large pieces of nuts remain. You may need to stop and scrape down the sides of the food processor a couple times.

Transfer this mixture to the cake tin and begin pushing down the cake base. The simplest way to do this is to fold the excess parchment over the base and use that to help press it down. This prevents your hands from getting sticky. I like to use a glass to press down on the parchment to really flatten it and make sure it is level. Place the base in the freezer while you work on the cream.

In a high-speed blender, add the strawberries, cashews, milk, maple syrup or coconut nectar, vanilla and pitaya powder and blend on high for a minute or until completely smooth and luscious. Pour the cashew cream over the base and smooth out using a spoon, spatula or simply by banging the tin on a counter a couple of times. Freeze for at least 2 hours, or overnight.

Top with gorgeous fresh berries before serving.

Note

Look for dates that have not been treated with sulfites!

Did You Know?

Dates are nature's candy! They're amazing for promoting bowel regularity, contain slow-release sugars, help maintain a regular heartbeat and soothe coughs and sore throats! Dates are immunity-boosting, a great source of potassium and contain protein and other essential nutrients like magnesium, manganese, selenium and zinc!

Nice Cream

SERVINGS: 2–3

This is nice (say in Borat accent) and it's made from bananas, other fresh fruits and no dairy! I don't know about you guys but even though I was addicted to Dairy Queen when I was young I would still approach near death every time I ate it because it upset my stomach that much! I later found out I have been allergic to dairy since I was a wee baby (Greek parents sometimes forget to tell you these things).

1 cup (175 g) Medjool dates

2 tbsp (26 g) coconut sugar

1 tsp vanilla

3 tbsp (45 ml) warm water

1 heaped tbsp (17 g) crunchy peanut butter

6 frozen bananas

¼ cup (60 ml) almond milk, unsweetened, from a carton

Chunks of Raw Brownies for Nanny Joan (page 174)

Coconut flakes

Cacao

Hemp seeds

Almond flakes

Blend the dates, coconut sugar, vanilla, warm water and peanut butter in a high-speed blender until creamy and delicious. Transfer the caramel mixture to a bowl and rinse the blender.

Blend the bananas and almond milk in the same high-speed blender until completely smooth and creamy like ice cream! You may need to add a little more almond milk to achieve the ice cream consistency but before you do, be patient and let the blender do its work. Use the tamper in the blender to push your bananas down to help with the process.

Top the nice cream with the caramel mixture and any of the optional toppings. Enjoy!

Did You Know?

Research shows that bananas on the riper end of the spectrum (think black spots!) contain a higher concentration of antioxidants and nutrients than their green counterparts. In addition to being sweeter, the riper a banana is the easier it is for the body to digest so this is something to try if you are prone to banana bloat.

Little Puffed Kamut Bars

SERVINGS: 6

Hey guys, welcome to the healthy and organic puffed wheat cakes recipe! I came up with this amazing simple recipe snack randomly. I was FaceTiming with Andrew while making it so it is genuinely a very intuitive/go-with-your-gut treat. I love making these for all occasions. They're great to snack on during road trips, after the gym or even as a dessert!

6 tbsp (30 g) cacao

6 tbsp (90 ml) coconut nectar

3 tbsp (45 ml) coconut oil, melted

3 tbsp (47 g) almond butter

5 cups (70 g) puffed kamut (can use puffed rice or anything puffed if you cannot find kamut)

Grease the mold of your choice with a bit of coconut oil (I use spray). I use 4¾ inch (12 cm) length, 1¹³⁄₁₆ inch (4.5 cm) width, ¾ inch (2 cm) height silicone molds.

In a large bowl combine the cacao, coconut nectar, coconut oil and almond butter. When the mixture is well-combined and smooth, add the puffed kamut and stir until completely covered. Transfer your mixture into your molds, flatten it with your fingers and freeze for about an hour before indulging! This is seriously simple and utterly incredible!

Did You Know?

Kamut is a high-energy and high-nutrient ancient grain! Many tests have been conducted on this beautiful ingredient but it is thought that kamut is the cousin to durum wheat. It is also known to be very easily digested, similar to bulgur wheat, and also has loads of protein; vitamins; minerals like zinc, magnesium and selenium; and amino acids. Kamut is a more nourishing alternative to traditional grains.

Nanny Matilde's Apple Crumble with a Twist

SERVINGS: 6

A few very special people in my life—my boyfriend and his two grandmothers—inspire this dish. Nanny Joan and Matilde are goddesses in the kitchen and little do they know they inspire me every time I get a chance to eat their baked goods. There is nothing in the world more comforting than a grandmother's touch and they show that through their cooking. I am so happy to include this in the book and I know all of you will love this simple, delicious and sweet treat! Enjoy this with your favorite vanilla ice cream.

8 royal gala apples, washed, cored and sliced (peeling is optional)

½ cup (100 g) coconut sugar

2 tbsp–¼ cup (28–55 g) dark brown organic sugar (add as much or as little as you'd like!)

1 tsp cinnamon

1 tsp vanilla

1 tbsp (8 g) flour (I used spelt flour)

5 tbsp (75 g) cold vegan butter, divided

1 cup (110 g) pecans

¾ cup (63 g) rolled oats

¼ cup (30 g) almond flour

⅓ cup (73 g) dark brown organic sugar

½ tsp vanilla

1 tsp cinnamon

½ tsp sea salt

Preheat the oven to 375°F (190°C). Lightly grease (I use coconut oil spray) an 11 x 6-inch (28 x 15-cm) pan.

Put the apples in a large bowl, along with the coconut sugar, brown sugar, cinnamon, vanilla and flour and stir. Put the apple mixture in the baking dish, spread evenly throughout. Dot the filling with 1 tablespoon (15 g) of butter, cut into small pieces, evenly spaced over the surface.

In a food processor, pulse the pecans until chunky. Don't overdo it; you want the crumble consistency to be quite textured. Transfer the pecans to a large mixing bowl and add the rolled oats, almond flour, brown sugar, vanilla, cinnamon and sea salt. Stir until well-combined. Add 4 tablespoons (60 g) of butter to the mixture and, using your hands, break it up until a crumble begins to develop. Pour the topping over the dish and distribute evenly. Bake for 40 minutes then broil for 5 minutes. You'll know it's ready when the filling is oozing and bubbly and your house smells like heaven.

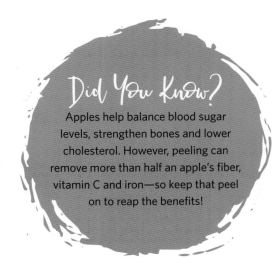

Did You Know?

Apples help balance blood sugar levels, strengthen bones and lower cholesterol. However, peeling can remove more than half an apple's fiber, vitamin C and iron—so keep that peel on to reap the benefits!

Hunger Bars SERVINGS: 12

This treat is unreal. I taste-tested this recipe once and that's all I needed. I had ten people try this treat and each and every person was pretty stoked about it; everyone asked for seconds and I don't think they left unsatisfied. Because this recipe has multiple steps, I suggest you only make this treat for special occasions or when you have extra time but hey, I can't stop you from making it any old time! The caramel is my favorite layer in this because I can eat a shit ton of it without having a panic attack worrying about eating something with no nutritional value.

2 cups (280 g) cashews

1 cup (120 ml) coconut cream, divided

⅓ cup (33 g) walnuts

¾ cup (180 ml) coconut oil, melted, divided

1 cup (240 ml) maple syrup, divided

¼ cup (29 g) almond meal

1½ tsp (7 ml) vanilla extract, divided

3 cups (525 g) Medjool dates

⅓ cup (83 g) almond butter

⅓ cup (95 g) peanut butter

1 tsp mesquite powder (this shit tastes like caramel goodness and I highly recommend investing in it!)

Sea salt

½ cup (40 g) cacao powder

Raw peanuts

Line an 8 x 8-inch (20 x 20-cm) cake tin with parchment (leave extra parchment hanging over on two sides, which will help you pat down the mixture). Have a cooling rack on hand.

Add the cashews, ½ cup (120 ml) of coconut cream, walnuts, ¼ cup (60 ml) of coconut oil, ¼ cup (60 ml) maple syrup, almond meal and 1 teaspoon vanilla to a high-speed blender and blend for 2 to 3 minutes or until completely smooth and silky. Transfer the mixture to the baking tin and flatten until it is even. The simplest way to do this is to fold the excess parchment over the base and use that to help press it down. This prevents your hands from getting sticky. I like to use a glass to press down on the parchment to really flatten it and make sure it is level. You could also spray a bit of coconut oil on a spatula and use this to press the mixture smooth. Place in the freezer while you make the caramel.

Add the dates, almond butter, peanut butter, ½ cup (120 ml) of coconut cream, ¼ cup (60 ml) of coconut oil, ¼ cup (60 ml) of maple syrup, mesquite powder, ½ teaspoon vanilla and salt to a high-speed blender and blend until completely smooth. The dates break down easily here but you still want to stay patient and blend for around 2 minutes to achieve a really silky effect. Pour this mixture over the nougat base and spread until flat and beautiful. Cover with parchment and set in the freezer for about 4 hours.

(continued)

HUNGER BARS (CONTINUED)

Remove the bars from the freezer and run a knife around the sides of the pan. Remove the bars from the pan set on a cutting board. Cut just centimeters from each side for a nice, square precise look (eat those bits you cut off, of course!) and then you're left to choose how you want to cut them into bars. I usually go for the longer/skinny look because they are quite thick. After you cut the bars put them back in the freezer while you prepare the chocolate.

Add ¼ cup (60 ml) of coconut oil to a saucepan and let it melt. Then add the cacao powder and ½ cup of maple syrup. Stir on low heat until combined. Remove from heat and when cool enough to handle, begin dipping your bars into the chocolate. Place the coated bars on a cooling rack and watch them dry up quickly! You can sprinkle some with peanuts and salt and some not. Have fun with these and do what you think your family will like most!

Did You Know?

Cacao powder is made by cold pressing the raw cacao beans, which means serious nutrition and benefits! Cold pressing removes the soft moisture (fat) and concentrates all the nutrients and enzymes. I love adding cacao powder to anything when I am craving that chocolaty taste!

Nourishing Carrot Cake with Vanilla Cashew Frosting

I never used to like carrot cake. That was until I tried my auntie's, then my cousin's and then I was hooked. I asked my cousin for the recipe and she gave it to me! I freaked out because at the time I was really afraid of food, so naturally when I saw that traditional carrot cakes have loads of "bad" oil, sugar and all-purpose flour I just couldn't believe that that's what I had been eating. I tried for a while to make it healthier by using olive oil, less sugar and different flours but then I said, fuck it. I can eat this with sugar but use less and I can use brown sugar and coconut sugar. I am not saying you can't re-create this recipe without sugar, what I am saying is that I decided I wanted to LIVE a little. Balance. I wanted balance and if that means I get to make this cake with sugar, coconut oil and some spelt flour then I will.

I know you're all going to love this recipe because I truly believe a part of my soul is really attached to it—it was one of the first recipes I created when I just coming into recovery from bulimia.

3 tbsp (23 g) ground flaxseed

¼ cup (60 ml) coconut oil, melted

1 cup (205 g) organic dark brown sugar

½ cup (128 g) applesauce

¾ cup (180 ml) almond milk

1 tsp apple cider vinegar

2 tsp (10 ml) vanilla

1 cup (115 g) almond meal

1 cup (120 g) spelt flour

1 tsp cinnamon

½ tsp salt

2 tsp (9 g) baking soda

1½ tsp (7 g) baking powder

2 cups (220 g) carrots, shredded, loosely packed

½ cup (55 g) crushed pecans

½ cup (47 g) unsweetened desiccated coconut

FROSTING

1¼ cups (175 g) raw cashews, soaked overnight or at least 4 hours

Juice of 1 lemon

3 tbsp (45 ml) pure maple syrup (use the best quality you can find)

2 tbsp (25 g) organic brown sugar

3 tbsp–½ cup (45–120 ml) nondairy milk

1–2 tsp vanilla extract

1 tsp cinnamon

Pinch of salt

Preheat the oven to 350°F (175°C) and line a 8- or 9-inch (20- or 23-cm) round baking pan with parchment or grease with coconut oil or butter.

To make the flax eggs, add 6 tablespoons (90 ml) of hot water to the flax in a small bowl and let sit for 5 minutes (watch as it thickens similar to the consistency of an egg).

(continued)

NOURISHING CARROT CAKE WITH VANILLA CASHEW FROSTING (CONTINUED)

In a large mixing bowl or stand mixer bowl add the coconut oil, brown sugar, applesauce, almond milk, vinegar and vanilla and blend *slowly*, until completely combined, but don't overdo it. If you're not using a stand mixer then simply use a hand mixer or spatula and the same rule applies: stir slowly! Add the flax mixture and gently stir.

In a separate medium-sized bowl, add the almond meal, spelt flour, cinnamon, salt, baking soda and baking powder. Stir until well-combined. Add the dry ingredients into the batter, stir to combine well, but again, be gentle and don't overdo it. Add shredded carrots, crushed pecans and coconut to the mixture and stir thoroughly. I like using a spatula for this part! Transfer the batter to the cake pan.

Bake for around 45 to 60 minutes; you will know when it's ready if you do the toothpick test. If it comes out clear then you're good! I love my cakes a tiny bit more dense and soft than traditionally made, so feel free to cook a bit longer to achieve what you like! Let cool completely.

Make the icing by combining the soaked cashews, lemon juice, maple syrup, brown sugar, milk, vanilla, cinnamon and salt in a high-speed blender and blend until smooth. Start with 3 tablespoons (45 ml) of milk and add more to reach desired consistency! You can also add a tad more salt if you want to adjust the sweetness.

When the cake is completely cooled, spoon the frosting on top.
Optional: Top with coconut or chopped walnuts!

Note

This frosting is less sweet than traditional carrot cake frostings so adapt as you please! You can also buy your favorite vegan frosting!

Did You Know?

The benefits of carrots are quite vast but their richness in beta-carotene takes the cake. A diet high in carotene helps decrease the incidence in some cancers! Carrots are also great for digestion, weight control, lowering cholesterol, strengthening your hair/nails and are even a great source for antioxidants. Other vegetables and fruits with carotene are: spinach, lettuce, tomatoes, sweet potatoes, broccoli, winter squashes and cantaloupe!

Peek-a-Boo Chickpea Fudge Bites   SERVINGS: 20

I know, I know, what kind of weirdo puts chickpeas into fudge? I do. I swear you can't taste them and they are super good! All you need here are 6 ingredients, 20 minutes and a little faith in the process. I remember when I first made these I was in shock about how interesting yet delicious they are! They're filled with plant-based protein, texture and character—I highly recommend them for snacks to have around the house when you need that extra pick-me-up!

1 (23.5-oz [398-ml]) can chickpeas, drained

½ cup (144 g) crunchy peanut butter or almond butter

½ cup (120 ml) maple syrup

2 tbsp–¼ cup (30–60 ml) almond milk

2 tsp (10 ml) vanilla

¼ cup (46 g) vegan chocolate chips

Line an 8 x 8-inch (20 x 20-cm) cake tin with parchment (leave extra on two sides to help you pat down the mixture).

In a food processor blend the chickpeas, peanut butter, maple syrup, almond milk and vanilla completely smooth. Start with the lower amount of milk and add more if necessary. You want to blend until you can no longer feel the grainy consistency of the chickpeas. Transfer the mixture into a medium-sized mixing bowl. Fold the chocolate chips into the "dough"-like fudge. Transfer to the baking pan, and using a flat surface like a coffee mug or spatula, even out the mixture until it is nice and flat.

Place the fudge in the freezer for up to 2 hours, then cut into chunks and enjoy. Store in an airtight container in the refrigerator or freezer!

Did You Know?

Chickpeas are incredible for our digestive system and bone health and here we are thinking only milk can save our bones! Hell, no—chickpeas can. They are rich in manganese, which helps build bones and is essential for bone structure. Chickpeas are also rich in calcium, phosphorus and magnesium. I think we all assume chickpeas are just for savory dishes but I think this dessert will help you see how versatile this beautiful pulse is!

Someone Give Me a Damn Chocolate Cake, Okay?

SERVINGS: 8

Holy guacamole, did someone say creamy chocolate cashew cheesecake? Yep, I did and this cake is entirely inspired by my childhood addiction. This cake is made using no sugar, no dairy, no bullshit—feel free to use organic food when you can—just straight-up goodness from the sweetness of dates. The crunch is from nuts like almonds and walnuts and the silky-smooth texture is from that crazy ingredient called CASHEWS and good-quality melted dark chocolate.

⅔ cup (100 g) dark chocolate

3 cups (525 g) pitted Medjool dates, soaked in warm water for 5 minutes

1 cup (138 g) raw almonds

1 cup (100 g) raw pecans

2 tbsp (30 ml) maple syrup

½ cup (120 ml) unsweetened coconut milk from carton

½ cup (120 ml) light coconut milk from can

1 tsp vanilla

3 cups (420 g) raw cashews

Fresh berries

Dark chocolate shavings

Lime zest

Fresh mint leaves

Line the base of a 9-inch (23-cm) springform pan with parchment.

Melt the chocolate in a microwave for about 20 seconds, or put it in a small bowl and set the small bowl in a shallow dish of hot water.

In a food processor, blend the dates, almonds, pecans and maple syrup until a large ball forms or until well-combined. You should still be able to see the nuts but make sure the dates are nice and smooth! Pour into the prepared pan and, using your hands, flatten out the dough. You can use the bottom of a cup or mug to make sure everything is even. Place in the freezer while you prepare the chocolate cheesecake.

Add the coconut milks, vanilla, melted chocolate and cashews to a high-speed blender and blend until smooth. This will take about 2 minutes. You may need to stop the blender and scrape down the sides of the blender a few times to make sure everything is well-blended. Transfer the mixture to the cake tin. A quick trick to flattening the cream is to slam the tin down on a counter or the table a couple times; it does the trick for me! If you have no stress to release, just use the back of a spoon to smooth it out. Place in the freezer to set for at least 3 hours (I prefer leaving it overnight).

Finish with fresh berries, chocolate, lime zest and mint as garnish. You can refer to my photo for inspiration!

This lasts in the freezer, covered with plastic wrap, for up to a week!

Did You Know?

Quality dark chocolate (with upwards of 70% cacao) is rich in the mineral iron. Iron is necessary for red blood cell production and a deficiency is associated with symptoms like extreme fatigue, brittle nails and headache.

Raw Brownies for Nanny Joan SERVINGS: 12

These gooey bite-sized brownies are exactly what you want and need if you are craving something sweet but really don't want the fuss of a 2-hour carrot cake or apple crumble. They are soft in texture, full-bodied in flavor and highly addicting. There's no need to worry about sugar or calories here (you shouldn't anyway), because they're sugar free and quite nourishing—thank you dates, walnuts and cacao. Crazy how nature's fruits can transform into something even more wonderful, eh?

4 cups (700 g) dates

2½ cups (250 g) walnuts + more for topping

½ cup (40 g) cacao powder

2 tbsp (30 ml) maple syrup

2 tbsp (30 ml) water

1 tsp vanilla

Pinch of sea salt

Line an 8 x 8-inch (20 x 20-cm) cake tin with parchment.

Blend the dates, walnuts, cacao powder, maple syrup, water, vanilla and salt in a high-speed blender or food processor until smooth, for around 3 minutes. This will seem like a long time but I promise you will not regret it! Transfer the brownie mixture into the baking dish and pat down with your hands until flat. Scatter walnuts on top and freeze for about 3 hours.

Cut into squares before enjoying with friends, family or just by yourself! ;)

Did You Know?

Cacao and cocoa may sound similar, but both of them are unique when it comes to nutrition, flavor and cost. Cacao is the purest form of chocolate that you can consume and is thought to be one of the highest sources of antioxidants of all foods. Being that it is closer to the original source, cacao is often more expensive than cocoa. Due to heavier processing, cocoa powder has less beneficial enzymes and a less acidic flavor.

Add Pizzazz to Your Food

There is no need to fear dressing, sauces and spreads! There is so much to learn and I'll be with you every step of the way.

Dressings, sauces and spreads were very confusing for me when I was young. I would always hear adults or older women talking about how they needed the "low-fat," "low-calorie" or "clear dressing" on their salad, veggies or bread. What the hell does any of this mean? Why light fat? Is fat bad? What are calories? Should I care? Should I count them? I DON'T KNOW!

Lucky for me, I grew up, suffered, learned and now I am here to share with you my favorite dressings, sauces and yummy goods that we make at home all the time and enjoy with a lot of our staple dishes! The word "guilt" should never be associated with food or eating so I am going to call these HAPPY SAUCES because guilt-free isn't a thing in my kitchen and it shouldn't be in yours either!

Strawberry Cashew Basil Dressing SERVINGS: 1

This dressing pairs well with leafy greens; nuts like walnuts and pecans; and citrus, dates and fruity salads! I love adding more pepper than usual, and if you do too then you'll find out why I am so obsessed!

1 cup (140 g) raw cashews

¼ cup (38 g) strawberries

¼ cup (10 g) basil, fresh

¼ cup (60 ml) lemon or lime juice

½ cup (120 ml) water

2 tbsp (30 ml) olive oil

Salt and pepper to taste

In a high-speed blender, blend the cashews, strawberries, basil, lemon or lime juice, water, olive oil and salt and pepper until smooth. I suggest doubling the recipe if you want to have more for later. It will keep in the refrigerator for up to 4 to 5 days!

In the Kitchen Tip

To keep your basil bright green in sauces, blanch the leaves for 5 seconds in boiling water to kill browning enzymes. Transfer to ice water for a quick "shock," pat dry with a paper towel and continue with the recipe.

Spicy Chili Peanut Butter Lime Dressing

SERVINGS: 1

This dressing doubles as a dip and damn it's da bomb! I love using it in all my Asian-inspired dishes, such as on my Summer Salad Rolls with Walnut Beef and Peanut Sauce (page 86) or my Easy Thai-Infused Coleslaw Salad (page 97)! The possibilities are pretty endless with this one but I also suggest trying it with stir fries, noodle dishes or even a dollop into a brothy soup—I know, weird, but it's amazing!

¼ cup (60 ml) olive oil

1 heaped tbsp (17 g) crunchy peanut butter (see Note)

1 tbsp (15 ml) hot sauce

1 tbsp (15 ml) soy sauce

Juice of 1 lime

1 clove garlic

½-inch (13-mm) cube of ginger

Dash of hot dried chilies

¼ cup (15 g) cilantro

½ cup (120 ml) water

Salt and pepper

In a high-speed blender or mason jar, blend/shake the olive oil, peanut butter, hot sauce, soy sauce, lime juice, garlic, ginger, chilies, cilantro, water and salt and pepper until you reach an even consistency. If you are using a mason jar instead of a blender, make sure to chop the garlic, ginger and cilantro ahead of time. I suggest doubling the recipe if you want to have more for later. This will keep in the refrigerator for up to 4 to 5 days!

*See photo on page 179.

Note

If you are making this recipe to use as a dipping sauce for the Summer Salad Rolls with Walnut Beef and Peanut Sauce (page 86), you may want to use more peanut butter for a chunkier sauce.

Did You Know?

Not a fan of spicy food? It might be worth getting used to it! Research shows that a tolerance to spicy foods can be built up over time and regular consumption may ward off disease and reduce pain associated with chronic illness.

Roasted Red Pepper & Sundried Tomato Dressing

This is a version of a classic without the crap but with all the goodness. I love using this as a dip for falafel, in salads using romaine and cabbage or even combined with fresh tomatoes and blended to make a lovely pasta sauce! This dressing is rich in nutrients, easy to make and sure to please the whole family.

1 red pepper, chopped

¼ cup (14 g) sundried tomatoes

¼ cup (35 g) roasted red peppers

1 tbsp (15 ml) extra virgin olive oil

¼ cup (60 ml) lemon juice

1 garlic clove

A few sprigs of fresh oregano

1 tbsp (15 g) Dijon mustard

Salt and pepper to taste

In a high-speed blender, blend the pepper, sundried tomatoes, roasted peppers, olive oil, lemon juice, garlic, oregano, mustard and salt and pepper until smooth. I suggest doubling the recipe if you want to have more for later. This lasts in the refrigerator for up to 4 days!

*See photo on page 179 and 182.

Did You Know?

A good extra virgin olive oil is an excellent source of polyphenols, antioxidants and vitamins K and E—but make sure you know what you're buying! Many olive oils these days are unfortunately blends and not made from 100% olives. Check the label and opt for a bottle that has been tinted— this is how the light-sensitive nutrients are protected by the seller, ensuring a higher quality product.

Creamy Greek "Feta" and Oregano Dressing
SERVINGS: 1

This one is a no-brainer! Add it to everything and live a happy life. I especially love adding this to quinoa Greek salads or anything with kale or loads of greens, like cucumber and parsley!

This dressing is on the thicker side, so if you add it to salads and know you usually fancy a lighter dressing, just add more water until you reach your preferred consistency!

½ cup (70 g) raw cashews

2 tbsp (30 ml) extra virgin olive oil

¼ cup (60 ml) lemon juice

1 cup (240 ml) water

1 tbsp (3 g) dried or fresh oregano

1 clove garlic

Salt and pepper to taste

½ tsp spirulina (optional)

In a high-speed blender, blend the cashews, olive oil, lemon juice, water, oregano, garlic and salt and pepper until smooth. I suggest doubling the recipe if you want to have more for later. This will keep in the refrigerator for up to 4 days!

Did You Know?

Long used by natural food companies as a food dye alternative, spirulina is a blue-green alga that strengthens the immune system, improves digestion and reduces inflammation. Available in powdered or tablet form (use the powdered form for this recipe!), spirulina is high in potassium, copper, magnesium, phosphorus, selenium and zinc and is also an excellent source of vitamins B, C, D, E and K.

the Nutella Imposter SERVINGS: 1

Oh Nutella, the memories that you bring me are beyond happy but I must admit . . . I was super pissed when I found out you were made of sugar and SINS!! In moderation, I might still consume you but I don't think I will ever again be smearing you over my toast for breakfast like I did when I was young.

I have nothing against sugar. I have nothing against bullshit ingredients. I am somewhat against the confusion caused by it all. There is a stigma and it needs to be shattered. I want you to know that everything in life is healthy—with balance. You don't have to create a restriction in your mind or a reason to not eat something simply because it's bad. That type of mindset really fucks with you and will eventually end up creating a type of eating disorder. I believe it is okay to eat what you want when you want as long as it makes you happy. Create knowledge around food and know your boundaries. If someone tells you Nutella is not healthy, you can't not agree with them, but if they try to tell you not to eat it you can tell them where to go and how to get there. This Nutella recipe can be consumed daily, enjoyed and eaten as you please.

1½ cups (173 g) raw hazelnuts

1 (13.5-oz [397-ml]) can full fat coconut milk

4 tbsp (20 g) cacao powder

⅓ cup (80 ml) maple syrup

1 tsp vanilla

Pinch of sea salt

2 tbsp (30 ml) coconut oil, melted

Preheat the oven to 375°F (190°C).

Toast the hazelnuts for 10 minutes on a baking sheet. Keep an eye on them so they don't burn. Remove them from the oven and when they have cooled slightly, use a cloth to rub them to try to remove as much skin as possible.

In a food processor, pulse the hazelnuts until a fine crumb develops.

Add the coconut milk, cacao powder, maple syrup, vanilla and salt to a large saucepan and stir over medium heat until well-combined. If you like your Nutella a little sweeter you can add more maple syrup but take into consideration that this will thin out the consistency, so do not add too much at once! Transfer the coconut/chocolate mixture to the food processor with the hazelnuts and blend until well-combined. Add the coconut oil and blend just one more time.

Store in a tightly sealed container in the refrigerator for up to 3 weeks.

Did You Know?

Hazelnuts are a wonderful source of folate and vitamin E. Folate is important for spine and brain development during pregnancy, and it helps slow brain-related degenerative diseases in adults.

Vegan Parmesan Cheese SERVINGS: 1

Yes, I said it: Vegan Parm that doesn't smell like feet but still tastes like magic. Made using versatile nutritional yeast, earthy nuts and simple seasonings. I don't really have too much else to say but I recommend you sprinkle this on everything! Note that you can also make this recipe using brazil nuts or cashews!

2 cups (200 g) walnuts (or cashews)

½ cup (144 g) nutritional yeast

½–1 tsp onion powder

½–1 tsp garlic powder

¾–1 tsp Himalayan salt

½ tsp fresh black pepper

Oregano, thyme or rosemary to taste (optional)

In a food processor, blend the walnuts, nutritional yeast, onion powder, garlic powder and salt and pepper until crumbs develop, about 20 to 25 seconds. This really does resemble Parmesan cheese so you will know when it's ready!

Did You Know?

Nutritional yeast is a deactivated yeast grown on molasses and is adored by the plant-based community for its uniquely cheesy flavor and vitamin profile. Sold in powder or flake form, nutritional yeast is filled with B vitamins, iron, zinc and it packs 9 grams of complete protein per tablespoon (18 g).

Butternut Squash No-Cheese Sauce SERVINGS: 4-6

This sauce is life changing! It's so good you can eat it with a spoon, in the tub, on a Tuesday. You have permission from me to enjoy this recipe at all times, anywhere you want. This stuff tastes *so* close to the real thing, doesn't require dairy and is packed with nutrients.

3 tbsp (45 ml) olive oil, divided

1 small butternut squash (or 4 cups [532 g] sweet potatoes, halved)

Salt and pepper

1 medium yellow onion, finely chopped

3 cloves garlic, pressed

½ cup (70 g) raw cashews

1 cup (240 ml) vegetable stock

½ cup (144 g) nutritional yeast

1 tsp paprika

½ tsp turmeric

Spoonful Dijon mustard

Juice of 1 large lemon

Preheat the oven to 375°F (190°C), line a baking sheet with parchment paper and drizzle with 1 tablespoon (15 ml) of olive oil, rubbing it around using your hands.

Halve the butternut squash lengthwise, remove the seeds, rub with 2 tablespoons (30 ml) of olive oil and season with salt and pepper. Bake, cut-side down for about 40 minutes, or until soft to touch with a fork. (If you are using sweet potato, follow these same instructions.)

While the squash is roasting, add a dash of olive oil to a cast-iron skillet and add the onion and garlic. Sauté them over medium heat until they are caramelized, about 10 to 15 minutes. Stir occasionally to avoid burning.

Add the cashews, stock, nutritional yeast, paprika, turmeric, Dijon, lemon and salt and pepper to a blender. Add the cooked onions to the blender and set aside.

When the squash (or sweet potato) is done, remove from the oven and once cool enough to handle, scoop out the insides and transfer to the blender. Begin by blending on low, then increase to high. If you are finding it difficult to blend, scrape down the sides and try to stay patient. When the mixture is smooth, transfer to a pot and reheat before enjoying with chips, veggies or preferably with pasta!

Creamy Roasted Cashew Nut Butter

SERVINGS: 3-4

Clearly the world is on a nut-butter kick and I thought I would quickly teach you all how to make that expensive goodness at home.

This recipe is super fun and easy to make, and you can use it in very creative ways! Smear on your toast; enjoy with fresh fruits; or even add it to your favorite homemade granola bars, energy bars or protein bites. For all you peanut butter lovers, this is a great substitute if you want to switch things up. Also, if you suffer from a peanut allergy then I highly recommend this. There's no need to deprive yourself, so when a recipe calls for PB then just change it up with CB!

4 cups (560 g) raw cashews

4 tbsp (60 ml) coconut oil, melted

Pinch of salt

1 tsp vanilla powder

1 tsp coconut sugar

Cacao, mesquite or cinnamon (optional)

Preheat the oven to 375°F (190°C) and line a baking sheet with parchment.

Spread the cashews on the baking sheet and bake for 10 minutes or until they are golden.

Transfer the cashews and coconut oil, salt, vanilla powder, coconut sugar and optional add-ins to a strong food processor and blend. At first, crumbs will develop, then the mixture will thicken. At this point you may think you are done, but keep blending until the natural oils release and the butter becomes runny and fabulous. You will not regret the extra time! This will take about 10 minutes.

Store in a jar or tightly sealed container in your pantry.

Note

You can use a high-speed blender to make this. The mixture will not be as smooth but it will still taste amazing!

Did You Know?

Cashew nut butter is a very rich source of essential minerals, especially copper. Dietary copper aids in the breakdown of fat in your food and is involved in the production of melanin and dopamine. Without enough copper, you can develop severe sunburn, chronic fatigue and other neurological disorders.

I'm Sorry Grandma, it's Vegan Cashew Tzatziki
SERVINGS: 3-4

Vegan tzatziki. Yep, I did it and before I dive into this recipe I feel like I owe an apology to my family. I must admit making this dip didn't feel right, it was like I was cheating on my Greek family . . . but then, I tried it. Oh my gosh, it's pretty damn close to the real deal and so flavorful. Suddenly my guilt evaporated and I was surprisingly happy that I made it!

This dish is traditionally vegetarian and often accompanies me at the table with all my vegetable recipes. I decided why not make it vegan and add it to my list of plant-based recipes that everyone MUST HAVE and I certainly do not regret it. It doesn't lack flavor, creaminess or strength. It's completely balanced with the amounts of fat, acidity and salt—I know you will love it!

1 cup (140 g) cashews soaked for at least 2 hours

¼ cup (60 ml) lemon juice

3 tbsp (45 g) sesame tahini

3 garlic cloves

½ cup (120 ml) water (add less or more to achieve preferred consistency)

Salt and pepper to taste

1 cup (140 g) cucumber, grated and squeezed to remove excess liquid

¼ cup (3 g) fresh dill, finely chopped

½ tbsp (1 g) mint, finely chopped (optional)

2–3 tbsp (30–45 ml) extra virgin olive oil

Add the cashews, lemon juice, tahini, garlic, water and salt and pepper to a food processor and blend until very smooth, scraping down the sides as necessary. Remove the mixture from the processor and transfer to a large mixing bowl. Add the cucumber, dill, mint and olive oil and stir until well-combined. Adjust the seasonings as desired.

Serve with salads, falafel, fresh veggies or your favorite crackers!

Store in a tightly sealed jar in your refrigerator for up to 1 week.

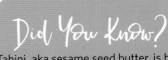

Did You Know?

Tahini, aka sesame seed butter, is high in trace minerals like zinc, which are needed to repair damaged tissue and produce collagen that gives skin its firmness and elasticity. Zinc also plays a role in immune system function and bone health.

Maria's Pantry

Here are some of the ingredients you can find in my pantry and throughout this cookbook. All very nourishing, versatile and great additions to your vegan/nonvegan cooking lifestyle.

ACAI POWDER

Acai powder is made from freeze-dried acai berries, a superfruit with a ton of health benefits. Acai berries have more antioxidants than any other fruit. They contain fiber and amino acids, plus high levels of essential fatty acids.

ARROWROOT POWDER

Arrowroot powder is a starch derived from a South American plant and is used as a thickener in recipes. I love it for thickening sauces because I don't use cheese!

ALMOND MEAL

Made from ground sweet almonds, almond meal has the consistency of corn meal and is a great substitute if you're gluten-free but still want a lot of flavor and texture in your baking.

ASHWAGANDHA

One of the most powerful herbs in Ayurvedic healing, ashwagandha is a superfood known for its restorative benefits.

BAOBAB

Baobab is a tree native to Africa, Madagascar, Australia and Arabia. It is used as a source of water and food for indigenous people. The fruit and leaves on this tree are used medicinally for things like mosquito repellent and treating asthma.

CACAO POWDER, RAW

This is the best chocolate substitute out there! Cacao is the purest form of chocolate you can consume. It's raw and significantly less processed than cocoa powder or most chocolate you find in a store. It's also high in antioxidants and magnesium!

CASHEWS

You'll need this ingredient to win the raw cake game! Cashews are rich in vitamin E and a good source of minerals like magnesium and zinc.

CHAGA

Known as the "king of medicinal mushrooms," this mushroom is filled with health benefits. Chaga is great for your immune system, can help fight diseases like cancer, reduces inflammation, is said to be anti-aging and the list goes on.

CHIA SEEDS

Chia seeds are known to be a brain food and can be great in puddings, breakfasts and used as a thickening agent while baking. They contain healthy omega-3 fatty acids, carbohydrates, protein, fiber and more.

CHICKPEA FLOUR

Used to make soy-free tofu and great for meatless meatballs and burgers, chickpea flour is gluten-free, and high in protein, iron and fiber.

COCONUT CREAM (COCONUT MILK)

This is a healthy substitute for traditional dairy cream. Coconut milk or cream has a consistency of cow's milk but instead is made from coconut. Because coconuts are loaded with health benefits, it's naturally a great alternative.

COCONUT OIL

Coconut oil can be great in recipes; it has a high smoking point, is a fantastic healthy fat and can even be used in various ways outside of the kitchen, too (like in your hair or on your skin). Coconut oil is well known for its wide array of health benefits and beauty routine uses. This healthy fat is unique in that it is an immediate source of energy when eaten and is not stored as fat within the body. Furthermore, coconut oil's unique array of fatty acids provide the body support in various functions from stabilizing hormone production, boosting the immune system and repairing damage in the gut caused by IBS.

COCONUT SUGAR

I am in love with coconut sugar! Coconut sugar retains nutrients found in the coconut palm. Regular sugar doesn't contain any nutrients, but coconut sugar has iron, zinc, calcium, antioxidants and more.

DATES

These are amazing if you want to make a recipe sugar-free. They also are loaded with flavor, vitamins and minerals and are a great source of energy. I use Medjool dates because they are softer and easier to blend than other varieties.

FARRO

Farro is a grain loaded with fiber; in fact, it has more fiber than other popular grains like rice or quinoa. Farro is supposed to improve digestion and cardiovascular health, plus it's filled with more than ten different vitamins and minerals.

FLAXSEEDS & FLAXSEED MEAL
Flaxseeds can be thrown into lots of recipes and really help with your digestion! Flaxseeds are loaded with omega-3 fatty acids, fiber and lignans (which has plant estrogen and antioxidant qualities).

MACA
Maca is another superfood that is loaded with more than twenty amino acids, twenty free-form fatty acids, vitamins, calcium and the list goes on and on. It can also be great for sexual health.

MESQUITE POWDER
This is used in my Hunger Bars recipe (page 165) because it tastes like caramel! Mesquite powder is made from dried and ground pods of mesquite and it's not only high in protein but contains goodness like calcium, magnesium, potassium and more.

NUTRITIONAL YEAST
Nutritional yeast is an excellent cheese substitute that's high in vitamin B12. It's also a complete protein and contains other B vitamins. The best part is, it's low in fat and sodium, plus free of sugar and gluten. Deficiency of vitamin B is usually associated with fatigue as it plays a big role in maintaining the health of the nervous system.

PITAYA POWDER
I love pitaya powder in watermelon juice for added nutrients and color. This bright pink powder comes from dragon fruit and is high in antioxidants. It's even been said to be beauty enhancing!

REISHI
Another mushroom and superfood, reishi is used for boosting your immune system and protecting it from the flu, lung conditions like asthma and more.

SPELT FLOUR
This amazing flour alternative is made from the delicious, easily digestible grain and is good for you, too. Spelt flour aids circulation, builds strong bones, boosts your immune system and that's just a few of the lengthy list of its attributes.

tools & Gadgets!

Here are the tools and gadgets I love using in the kitchen. Perfect for raw treats, elixirs and gorgeous cakes!

FOOD PROCESSOR

My Kitchen Aid food processor is my fave! When picking a food processor for your kitchen, it's important to choose a good-quality one; however, don't break the bank. My food processor is used for almost everything and is a critical tool for developing a strong plant-based diet.

HIGH-SPEED BLENDER

The rule of thumb for choosing a blender is the stronger the better. I use a Vitamix blender and it's perfect for blending cashews and making all the drinks, cakes and treats.

STAND MIXER

My Kitchen Aid stand mixer is fun to use and really helps you in the kitchen. Pizza, bread and cakes will never be the same once you have one of these! Because a lot of people don't already have a mixer in their kitchen, you won't see it mentioned in a lot of my recipes; however, you can use it where you see fit!

POTS & PANS

I use Staub, Le Crueset and Padorna. You want to ensure that whatever pots or pans you're using, they are nonstick and goo resistant! This will make cooking easy, plus they'll be much easier to clean.

SILICON MOLDS

Silicon molds can be a great addition to your kitchen, especially when making raw cakes and muffins. Using silicon instead of regular pans can make removal easier and your end product more presentable.

SPRINGFORM PAN

A springform pan is a necessity for perfect cakes. I strongly suggest you add one of these to your kitchen, especially if you love to bake. With a springform pan, the sides are removable, which makes for beautiful, presentable cakes that will wow your guests!

Shopping List

I realize these lists might seem intimidating, but here's the thing, once you have them, you have them! You'll be more inclined to try new things and you'll probably feel a lot better too! I used to ponder how people could have a fully stocked pantry of goodness but now I understand . . . because when you do, the possibilities really become endless!

FOR THE REFRIGERATOR

- Apples
- Avocado
- Beets
- Broccoli and Broccolini
- Butternut squash
- Carrots
- Cucumber
- Eggplant
- Eggs
- Feta
- Figs
- Lemons and limes
- Lettuce, kale and spinach
- Mushrooms
- Oranges
- Peppers
- Spaghetti squash
- Trout
- Zucchini

WITHIN ARM'S REACH

- Apple cider vinegar
- Bananas
- Black pepper
- Brown rice syrup
- Coconut oil
- Extra virgin olive oil
- Fresh cilantro, dill, mint, parsley and basil
- Maple syrup
- Sea salt
- Sourdough bread
- Tomatoes

FREEZER

- Bananas
- Berries
- Kale
- Spinach

DRY PANTRY GOODS

- Almond meal
- Almonds
- Arrowroot powder
- Assorted beans
- Assorted onions
- Assorted pastas and rice noodle products
- Barley
- Brown, arborio and jasmine rice
- Bulgur
- Cashews
- Chia seeds
- Chickpea flour
- Chickpeas
- Couscous
- Farro
- Flaxseeds
- Garlic
- Hazelnuts
- Lentils
- Nutritional yeast
- Organic vegetable stock cubes
- Pecans
- Potatoes
- Puffed quinoa and kamut
- Pumpkin seeds
- Quinoa
- Rolled oats
- Sunflower seeds
- Superfoods: matcha, acai, cacao
- Tahini
- Walnuts

Acknowledgments

It seems like only yesterday that I had this little dream to share my story about my battle with bulimia—I dreamed of helping people all around the world. There are so many people that I have to thank for helping me fall onto this path. You are all so amazing and without you, none of this would have happened!

My rock. Thank you, Andrew, for dealing with me the whole summer I was writing this cookbook—I was a crazy person and you loved me regardless. I don't give you enough credit because let's be honest, I'm not the type of woman to admit I need help. We didn't just meet because we were meant for each other. We met because you were brought to me to help me get better. I beat bulimia because I am strong but you helped build a strong base for self-love, acceptance and lots of courage. We are an amazing team Andrew and I am so thankful for you.

Thank you so much to Page Street Publishing for making my dreams come true! Will and Marissa, you are both one of a kind, you are amazing. It was a month before I received your email that I had changed my Instagram biography to read "Author." I wasn't an author yet but I knew one day that my dreams would come true! It was a sign when I received that email, the email that will forever change my life. Thank you so much for believing in me and for letting me share my story and help people all around the world.

Thank you to my mom, dad, sister and brother. Thank you for dealing with me when I didn't pay the rent. Thank you for yelling at me when you knew I could do better. Thank you for challenging my thoughts and for helping me dig deeper. Thank you for supporting me, loving me and being there even when we were oceans, hours and area codes apart.

Thank you, Caitlin, for believing in me, for helping me start this dream. For being patient and for literally creating the blog I could only dream about. We had no idea this would happen just two short years ago but somehow, we did it!

Thank you to my friends for your support. In a world this busy it is hard to find people like you. You all know who you are and I cannot wait to celebrate this moment in my life with all of you by my side.

Thank you to my followers for your love and for following my blog and my Instagram! Without you, none of this would be possible. You helped me grow a platform that allows me to change the lives of thousands of people. I love each of you so much.

Thank you @co.create.co, @farmhousepottery, @beckydaisym and @as.ceramics for your beautiful ceramics that I was so lucky to use throughout the photography and styling of this book. Thank you @christopheramat for the lifestyle shots, they turned out better than I imagined. Thank you to my sister, @konstantineclothing for your gorgeous linen white jumper and @hazelandfolk for the dress worn on the cover. Last but not least, thank you @eclectic.lab.designs for your food photography backdrops! I love using them!

I CANNOT THANK YOU ALL ENOUGH!